Mates in Chelsea

Rory Mullarkey

methuen | drama

LONDON • NEW YORK • OXFORD • NEW DELHI • SYDNEY

METHUEN DRAMA
Bloomsbury Publishing Plc
50 Bedford Square, London, WC1B 3DP, UK
1385 Broadway, New York, NY 10018, USA
29 Earlsfort Terrace, Dublin 2, Ireland

BLOOMSBURY, METHUEN DRAMA and the Methuen
Drama logo are trademarks of Bloomsbury Publishing Plc

First published in Great Britain 2023

A catalogue record for this book is available from the British Library.

A catalog record for this book is available from the Library of Congress.

ISBN: PB: 978-1-3504-4835-3
ePDF: 978-1-3504-4837-7
eBook: 978-1-3504-4836-0

Series: Modern Plays

Typeset by Mark Heslington Ltd, Scarborough, North Yorkshire

To find out more about our authors and books visit
www.bloomsbury.com and sign up for our newsletters.

THE ROYAL COURT THEATRE PRESENTS

Mates in Chelsea

by Rory Mullarkey

Mates in Chelsea was first performed at the Royal Court Jerwood
Theatre Downstairs, Sloane Square, on Friday 3 November 2023.

Mates in Chelsea

by Rory Mullarkey

Cast (in alphabetical order)

Mrs Hanratty **Amy Booth-Steel**
Finty Crossbell **Natalie Dew**
Simone Montesquieu **Karina Fernandez**
Charlton Thrupp **George Fouracres**
Theodore 'Tug' Bungay **Laurie Kynaston**
Oleg Mikhailovich Govorov **Philipp Mogilnitskiy**
Agrippina Bungay **Fenella Woolgar**

Director **Sam Pritchard**
Designer **Milla Clarke**
Lighting Designer **Natasha Chivers**
Sound Designer **Christopher Shutt**
Movement Director **Malik Nashad Sharpe**
Assistant Director **Aneesha Srinivasan**
Dialect Coach **Penny Dyer**
Fight Director **Bret Yount**
Production Manager **Vivienne Clavering**
Stage Manager **Chris Peterson**
Deputy Stage Manager **Julia Slienger**
Assistant Stage Manager **Tash Savidge**
Stage Management Work Placement **Julia Wilkens**
Show Crew **Oscar Sale**
Sound Operator **Florence Hand**
Dressers **Alex Papachristou-Cox & Milla Tikkanen**
Alterations **Anna Barcock**
Special Effects **Erin Jacques**
Wigs Supervisor **Carole Hancock**
Set built by **Footprint Scenery**
Artist support by **The Artist Wellbeing Company**

From the Royal Court, on this production:

Casting Directors **Amy Ball & Arthur Carrington**
Stage Supervisors **TJ Chappell-Meade & Steve Evans**
Lighting Supervisors **Max Cherry & Deanna Towli**
Stage Show Technician **Maddy Collins**
Lead Producer **Chris James**
Sound Supervisors **David McSeveney & Jet Sharp**
Lighting Programmer **Lucinda Plummer**
Company Manager **Mica Taylor**
Costume Supervisor **Lucy Walshaw**

The Royal Court Theatre and Stage Management wish to thank the following for their help with this production:
Sir Chris Bryant MP, Gavanndra Hodge, Lola Kezunovic.

Rory Mullarkey (Writer)

For the Royal Court: **Pity, The Wolf from the Door, Remembrance Day [translation].**

Other theatre includes: **Wintry Tales (Live, Newcastle); Saint George & the Dragon (National); Each Slow Dusk (Pentabus/UK tour); Cannibals, Single Sex (Royal Exchange, Manchester); Flood (NYT); The Grandfathers (NT Connections/Bristol Old Vic/National); On the Threshing Floor (Heat&Light Company/Hampstead).**

Adaptations/translations include: **The Cherry Orchard (Bristol Old Vic/Royal Exchange, Manchester); The Oresteia (Globe).**

Libretti include: **The Skating Rink (Garsington); Coraline (Royal Opera House); The Way Back Home (ENO/Young Vic).**

Awards include: **Abraham Woursell Prize; Harold Pinter Commission; George Devine Award; James Tait Black Prize for Drama.**

Amy Booth-Steel
(Mrs Hanratty)

Theatre includes: **The Odyssey, Dick Whittington, A Pacifist's Guide to the War on Cancer (& Complicité), The Light Princess, One Man, Two Guvnors, She Stoops to Conquer (National); Assassins (Chichester Festival Theatre); Tammy Faye (Almeida); The Magician's Elephant (RSC); #HonestAmy (Pleasance, Edinburgh); Heathers, Sister Act, The Sound of Music (West End); As You Like It (Regent's Park Open Air); The Assassination of Katie Hopkins (Theatr Clwyd); Anita & Me (Birmingham Rep and Royal Stratford East); The Secret Diary of Adrian Mole (Leicester Curve); Betty Blue Eyes (Mercury/West Yorkshire Playhouse); Swallows and Amazons (Bristol Old Vic).**

Television includes: **Late in Life, One Day, Nolly, Stath Lets Flats, The Mind of Herbert Clunkerdunk, Buffering, Call the Midwife, Close to Me, Newark Newark, Zomboat, Doctor Who, The Year of the Rabbit, Wannabe, Coronation Street, The Windsors, Doctors.**

Film includes: **Blue Jean.**

Natasha Chivers
(Lighting Designer)

For the Royal Court: **Shoe Lady, White Pearl, Inside Bitch (& Clean Break), The Cane, Bad Roads, Fireworks, Adler & Gibb, The Mistress Contract, Gastronauts, The Djinns of Eidgah, That Face (& West End).**

Other theatre includes: **Prima Facie (West End/Broadway/NT Live); Sylvia (Old Vic); The Doctor, Hamlet, Orestela (New York/West End/Almeida); Judas, Oedipus (Toneelgroep, Amsterdam); Antipodes, Sunset at the Villa Thalia, Statement of Regret (National); Ivanov (Staatstheater Stuttgart); Blood Wedding (Young Vic); Allelujah (Bridge/NT Live); The Duchess of Malfi (RSC); 1984 (West End/Broadway); The House They Grew Up In (Chichester Festival); Happy Days (Crucible, Sheffield); Green Snake (National Theatre of China); The Radicalisation of Bradley Manning (National Theatre Wales); Macbeth (& Broadway); 27, The Wolves in the Walls, Home (National Theatre of Scotland).**

Dance includes: **Peaky Blinders: The Redemption of Thomas Shelby (Rambert); Message in a Bottle (Sadler's Wells); Aisha & Abhaya Linbury Rambert/Linbury Theatre; Belonging (Skånes Dansteater, Sweden); Strapless, Electric Counterpoint (Royal Ballet).**

Awards include: **Drama Desk Award (Prima Facie), Olivier Award for Best Lighting Design (Sunday in the Park with George), Theatre Award UK for Best Design (Happy Days).**

Milla Clarke (Designer)

As designer, for the Royal Court: **Inside Bitch (& Clean Break), Bad Roads, Human Animals.**

As associate designer, for the Royal Court: **B, Victory Condition.**

As designer, other theatre includes: **Cat on a Hot Tinned Roof (Royal Exchange); Macbeth (Reykjavik City); Bootycandy, A Small Place (Gate); Red Ellen (Northern Stage); Ivy Tiller: Vicar's Daughter, Squirrel Killer, and O, Island! (RSC); Isla (Theatr Clwyd); The Brief and Frightening Reign of Phil [co-designed with Chloe Lamford](New Zealand Festival Theatre); Yolk and Aliens [co-created with Jane Horrocks, Molly Vivian and Francesca Levi] (Brighton Festival); Curious [co-designed with Rosie Elnile] (Soho); Elephant (Birmingham Rep); Outside and Out of Water (Orange Tree); Yuri (Chapter, Cardiff); Wind Resistance (Lyceum, Edinburgh); Seagulls (Volcano).**

As designer, opera includes: **La Traviata (Nevill Holt); La Bohème (ENO: Drive & Live); The Day After, Trial by Jury (ENO).**

Awards include: **Linbury Prize for Stage Design; Lord Williams Prize for Design; The Prince of Wales Design Scholarship.**

Vivienne Clavering
(Production Manager)

Theatre includes: **Death of England: Closing Time, The Odyssey, Connections Festival, Shut up I'm Dreaming, A Winter's Tale (National); Susanna, Aisha and Abaya, The Lost Thing, Phaedra, Berenice (Royal Opera House); The Gretchen Question (Fuel); The Promise (Handpicked Productions/Tour); Playground Victories (Scribbled Thought/Tour); SEND Show (Young Vic); I Told my Mum I was on a RE Trip (20 Stories Hight/Contact/Tour); Tomorrow I Was A Lion (Belarus Free Theatre/Tour); Full Stop (Lyric Hammersmith/Light The Fuse/Tour); And Yet It Moves, The Space Between (The Young Vic Theatre), Chalk Farm (ThickSkin/Edinburgh Festival/Cultura Inglesa Festival/Sao Paulo/Brits off Broadway/59E59 Theater New York); A Tender Thing, Beauty and the Beast, I Was A Wife, Stones in His Pockets, The Crucible (Dukes Playhouse), Mare Rider (Arcola/European Tour).**

Natalie Dew (Finty Crossbell)

For the Royal Court: **Human Animals, Teh Internet is Serious Business, Rough Cuts.**

Other theatre includes: **The Provoked Wife and Venice Preserved, Arabian Nights (RSC); Twelfth Night (Young Vic); Deposit (Hampstead); Breaking the Code (Royal Exchange); Bend It like Beckham,(West End); Twelfth Night (Liverpool Everyman); Fault Lines (Hampstead); Romeo & Juliet (National);Hamlet (Northern Broadsides); As You Like It (Leicester Curve); Hansel &Gretel (Barbican); Twelfth Night (Regents Park).**

Television includes: **Bodies, Alex Rider, Archer, The Capture, Sandylands, The Great, Roadkill, Bodyguard, Kiri, Gavin & Stacey.**

Penny Dyer (Dialect Coach)

For the Royal Court: **The Wolf From The Door, Linda, The Mistress Contract, Circle Mirror Transformation, The Low Road, Choir Boy, In Basildon, Posh (& West End), Clybourne Park (& West End), The Faith Machine, The Girlfriend Experience, Chicken Soup with Barley, Aunt Dan & Lemon, The Fever, Tusk Tusk, Wig Out! The Pride, Now or Later, The Vertical Hour, Redundant, Plasticine, Spinning into Butter, Fireface, Other People, Mojo (& West End).**

Other theatre includes: **Groundhog Day, Eureka Day, Faith Healer, A Very Expensive Poison, Present Laughter, The American Clock, Girl from the North Country, A Christmas Carol, The Caretaker (Old Vic); Heisenberg, A Long Day's Journey Into Night, Who's Afraid of Virginia Woolf, Gypsy, Good People, The Commitments, Posh (West End); When Winston Went to War with the Wireless, Roots, Teddy Ferrara (Donmar); The Corn is Green, The Normal Heart, Follies, The Red Barn, Husbands and Sons, This House, Blood & Gifts (National).**

Television includes: **The Post Office vs Mr Bates, Curveball, Debutante, Mammals, Wednesday, Becoming Elizabeth, Belgravia, White House Murders, Pure, Hanna, Patrick Melrose, Urban Myths, The Rack Pack, Marvellous, Cilla, Tommy Cooper, The Girl, Mrs Biggs, The Deal.**

Film includes: **The Tutor, Matilda the Musical, After Love, The Mauritanian, The Courier, On Chesil Beach, The Danish Girl, Florence Foster Jenkins, Pride, Philomena, Infamous, Frost Nixon, The Queen, The Damned United, Dirty Pretty Things, The War Zone, Elizabeth.**

Karina Fernandez
(Simone Montesquieu)

For the Royal Court: **Blue Heart (& Out of Joint).**

Other theatre includes: **Fanny and Alexander (Old Vic); Shrapnel: 34 Fragments of a Massacre, Mare Rider (& Podium Mozaiek), Gibraltar (Arcola); Double Feature (National); The Convicts' Opera (& Sydney Theatre Company), Shopping and F***king (& G & J Prods) (Out of Joint); Wedding Day at the Cro-Magnons (Soho); Macbeth (Bristol Old Vic); Mrs Pat (Theatre Royal, York); Crocodile Seeking Refuge (Lyric Hammersmith and Ice and Fire); Woody Allen's Murder Mysteries (Croydon Warehouse); Bites (Bush/Mama Quillo); Hamlet (Wild Thyme); Passion (Chelsea Theatre); Dealing with Claire (Union); Romeo & Juliet (UK tour); The Boy Who Left Home (ATC); Cool Water Murder (Coventry Belgrade Theatre); Trips (Birmingham Rep).**

Television includes: **The Thief, His Wife and the Canoe, Killing Eve, Trying, Holby City, A Young Doctor's Notebook, A Touch of Cloth, Falcon, Twenty Twelve, Married Single Other, My Family, My So-Called Life Sentence, The Forsyte Saga, Happy Birthday Shakespeare, Quick Cuts.**

Film includes: **Miss Marx, The One and Only Ivan, Nico 1988, Daphne, The Sense of an Ending, Pride, Mr Turner, Now is Good, Another Year, Happy Go Lucky, The Return, Gabriel.**

Radio includes: **Welcome to Iran, Plum House – Lights Camera Pudding, Brave New World, Rock Me Amadeus.**

George Fouracres
(Charlton Thrupp)

Theatre includes: **The Comedy of Errors, The Tempest, Much Ado About Nothing, Hamlet, Twelfth Night, A Midsummer Night's Dream (Globe); A Midsummer Night's Dream (Filter Theatre) The Diary of a Nobody (Rough Haired Pointer); Scrooge & Marley (Dippermouth) Television includes: Don't Hug Me I'm Scared, Semi-Detached, Spitting Image, Whiskey Cavalier, Pls Like, Comic Relief, Drunk History, Raised by Wolves, The Scandalous Lady W.**

Film includes: **Accident Man: Hitman's Holiday.**

Comedy includes: **George Fouracres: Gentlemon, The 'Best' of Daphne, Daphne in the Moonlight, Daphne's Second Show, Daphne Do Edinburgh, Nova! Nova!**

Radio includes: **George Fouracres: Black Country Gentlemon, The Now Show, Alexei Sayle's Absence of Normal, The Wilsons Save the World, The Lenny Henry Show, Always June, Claire in the Community, Vip Rip, Eastenders: The Podcast, Britain in Bits with Ross Noble, Jake Yapp's Media Circus, Lenny Henry's Rogues Gallery, Daphne Sounds Expensive, Spotlight Tonight with Nish Kumar, Newsjack.**

Laurie Kynaston
(Theodore 'Tug' Bungay)

For the Royal Court: **The Ferryman (& West End).**

Theatre includes: **Spring Awakening (Almeida); The Son (Kiln/West End); Elegies for Angels, Punks and Raging Queens (Charing Cross); Jumpy, The Winslow Boy (Theatr Clwyd); This Smudge Won't Budge (The Other Palace).**

Television includes: **A Small Light, Fool Me Once, The Doll Factory, The Sandman, Life After Life, The Man Who Fell to Earth, Des, The Split, When Barbara Kissed Joan – Urban Myths, The Trouble With Maggie Cole, Derry Girls, The Feed, Cradle to Grave, Murder Games: the Life and Death of Breck Bednar, Doctors, Our World War, Casualty.**

Film includes: **How to Build a Girl, Muse, Nocturnal, Intrigo: Dear Agnes, Undercliffe, England is Mine, Gloves Off, They Found Hell, Gutterdämmerung.**

Radio includes: **The Son, What Does the K Stand For?**

Awards include: **WhatsOnStage Award Best Actor Nominee (The Son), Evening Standard Award for Emerging Talent (The Son), Screen International Star of Tomorrow.**

Philipp Mogilnitskiy
(Oleg Mikhailovich Govorov)

For the Royal Court: **two Palestinians go dogging.**

Other theatre includes: **Iran Conference (Weda, Warsaw); The Trials of John Demjanjuk: A Holocaust Cabaret (Confrontation Festival); The Face of Jizo (Ethud); Brothers & Sisters, An Enemy of the People, Gaudeamus, Life & Fate, Our Class (Maly Drama, St. Petersburg); The Pillowman (On Theatre).**

Television includes: **The Thaw, Furia, Dom Pod Dwoma Orlami, Into The Night, Król, S'parta, Zluk: The Young Pilsudski, De 12 Van Schouwendam, Maly Zgon, Nielegalni, Podkidysh, Ulyotnyy Ekipazh, Full Moon, Krylya Imperii, Ne Vmeste, Takaya Rabota, Svoya Chuzhaya, Morskie Dyavoly: Smerch 2, Desant Est Desant, Voennaya Razvedka: Zapadnyy Front, Ottsy, Liteynyy, Tayny Sledstviya.**

Film includes: **Lucky Man, Shtti, Minsk, What the French Keep Still About, Zatopek.**

Chris Peterson
(Stage Manager)

For the Royal Court: **Killology (& Sherman).**

Other theatre includes: **The SpongeBob Musical (UK & Ireland Tour); & Juliet (West End); Painkiller, After The End (Stratford East).**

As company stage manager, theatre includes: **House of Shades, Once Upon A Time in Nazi-Occupied Tunisia (Almeida); Peter Pan, Dick Whittington (Crossroads Pantomimes); Beyond These Walls (Northern Broadsides); Dumb Waiter (Hampstead); Captain Corellis Mandolin (UK Tour/West End); Two Trains Running (ETT/ Royal and Derngate); Billionaire Boy (Nuffield/ UK Tour); Fup (Kneehigh/UK Tour); Tremor, Dublin Carol, Wind In The Willows, The Cherry Orchard, The Borrowers, The Weir (& Tobacco Factory), The Hunting of the Snark (& RGM), Bird (& Royal Exchange),The Lion, The Witch and the Wardrobe, A Doll's House (Sherman).**

Sam Pritchard (Director)

For the Royal Court: all of it (& Avignon Festival), A Fight Against... (Una Lucha Contra...), Living Newspaper, Pity, Grimly Handsome [co-creator], B.

Other theatre includes: The Mysteries, Galka Motalka (Royal Exchange, Manchester); Pygmalion (Headlong/Leeds Playhouse/Nuffield/UK tour); There Has Possibly Been an Incident (Royal Exchange, Manchester/Soho/Edinburgh Festival Fringe/Theatertreffen, Berlin); Fireface (Young Vic).

Sam was the winner of the JMK Award for Directors in 2012. He is the Associate Director (International) at the Royal Court.

Tash Savidge
(Assistant Stage Manager)

Theatre includes: Love (Park Avenue Armory NYC/Vienna Arts Festival); Jesus Christ Superstar, Evita (Regent's Park Open Air); The Visit, The Lehman Trilogy, Amadeus, The Suicide, Wonder.land, Jane Eyre (National); The Convert (Young Vic), Pink Mist (Bristol Old Vic).

As stage manager, theatre includes: The Walk (Good Chance); For All The Women... (Stoke Newington Town Hall); Human Jam (Camden People's); Broad Shadow (National).

Malik Nashad Sharpe
(Movement Director)

For the Royal Court: The Glow, Living Newspaper.

Other theatre includes: Henry V (& Globe), A View from the Bridge (& Chichester Festival / Bolton Octagon) Headlong); Bootycandy, Effigies of Wickedness (& ENO) (Gate); Closer, Scandaltown (Lyric Hammersmith); Two-Character Play (Hampstead); Fairview (Young Vic).

As choreographer, theatre includes: High Bed Lower Castle [co-created with Ellen Furey] (Festival Transamerique); DARK, HAPPY, to the CORE (Roskilde Festival).

Awards include: Simone Michele Prize for Outstanding Choreography.

In 2019, Malik was named a Rising Star in Dance from Attitude Magazine, and in 2022, was featured on the prestigious Forbes 30 under 30 list for his unique and pervasive choreographic achievements. In 2023, he was nominated for the Premio Cunha e Silva Prize at Galeria Municipal do Porto.

Malik is currently an Associate Artist at The Place, and a studio resident of Somerset House Studios. He has held artistic residencies at Sadlers Wells, Barbican, Performance Situation Room, Dance4, Duckie, and Tate Modern. He is currently a guest teacher in dance and performance at the Stockholm University of the Arts in Sweden.

Christopher Shutt
(Sound Designer)

For the Royal Court: Glass. Kill. Bluebeard. Imp., a profoundly affectionate, passionate devotion to someone (-noun), Escaped Alone, The Sewing Group, hang, Love & Information (& Minetta Lane, NYC), Kin, Aunt Dan & Lemon, Bliss, Free Outgoing, The Arsonists, Serious Money, Road.

Other theatre includes: Drive Your Plow Over the Bones of the Dead, A Disappearing Number, The Elephant Vanishes, Mnemonic, The Noise of Time, The Street of Crocodiles, The Three Lives of Lucie Cabrol, The Caucasian Chalk Circle (Complicité); Brokeback Mountain, The Entertainer, The Winter's Tale (West End); The Crucible, Paradise, Hansard, Antony & Cleopatra, Julie, John, Twelfth Night, Here We Go, The Beaux Stratagem, Man & Superman, The James Plays (I & II), From Morning to Midnight, Strange Interlude, Timon of Athens, The Last of the Haussmans, The White Guard, Burnt by the Sun, Every Good Boy Deserves Favour, The Hour We Knew Nothing of Each Other, War Horse (& West End), Happy Days, Thérèse Raquin, The Seagull, Burn/Chatroom/Citizenship, Coram Boy, A Minute Too Late, Play Without Words, Machinal (National); Aristocrats, Saint Joan, Faith Healer, St Nicholas, Privacy, Philadelphia Here I Come!, Piaf, The Man Who Had All the Luck (Donmar); Nightfall (Bridge); Wild, A Human Being Died That Night, And No More Shall We Part, For Once (Hampstead); The Merchant of Venice (Globe); The Father (& Theatre Royal, Bath/West End), The Caretaker (& Crucible, Sheffield) (Kiln); Hamlet (Barbican); Bull (Young Vic); The Playboy of the Western World, All About My Mother, Life x 3 (Old Vic); The Clinic, Ruined, Judgement Day (Almeida); Desire Under the Elms, Blasted (Lyric, Hammersmith); Thyestes (Arcola); Shoes (Sadler's Wells); Julius Caesar (Barbican); Oppenheimer (& West End), Macbeth, The Two Gentlemen of Verona, Wendy & Peter Pan, Twelfth Night, The Comedy of Errors, The Tempest, King Lear, Romeo & Juliet, Noughts & Crosses (RSC); Macbeth (Manchester International Festival/New York); Drum Belly (Abbey); Crave/4:48 Psychosis (Sheffield Theatres); Far Away, A Midsummer Night's Dream (Bristol Old Vic); Good (Royal Exchange, Manchester); Man of Aran (Druid, Galway); Murder on the Orient Express, Country Girls, The House of Special Purpose (Chichester Festival); Little Otik, The Bacchae (National Theatre of Scotland); Riders to the Sea (ENO); A Human Being Died That Night, Macbeth, All My Sons, The Resistible Rise of Arturo Ui, Happy Days, A Moon for the Misbegotten, Coram Boy, Humble Boy, Not About Nightingales, Mnemonic (Broadway).

Awards include: **Tony Award for Best Sound Design of a Play (War Horse); New York Drama Desk Award for Outstanding Sound Design (Mnemonic, Not About Nightingales).**

Julia Slienger
(Deputy Stage Manager)

For the Royal Court: **A Fight Against... (Una Lucha Contra...), Scenes with girls, The Woods, My Mum's A Twat, Grimly Handsome, Victory Condition, Road, Torn, Unreachable, I See You (& Market Theatre Johannesburg/Fugard Cape Town), You For Me For You, Who Cares, Fireworks, The Mistress Contract, The Djinns Of Eidgah, Talk Show, Collaboration, The President Has Come To See You, Narrative, No Quarter, Vera Vera Vera, The Westbridge, A Separate Reality, The Village Bike.**

Other theatre includes: **The Confessions (Wiener Festwochen/Athens Epidaurus Festival/Grec Festival/Festival D'Avignon/Odéon Théâtre de l'Europe); Love (Park Avenue Armory); Good (Harold Pinter); A Christmas Carol-ish (Soho); Reason's You Should(n't) Love Me (Kiln); Invisible Cities (MIF/Brisbane Festival); Absolute Hell (National); A Midsummer Night's Dream, Measure For Measure, The Changeling (Young Vic); Shipwreck, Little Revolution (Almeida); A Human Being Died That Night (Hampstead/BAM); Praxis Makes Perfect (Berlin Festspiele).**

As stage manager, theatre includes: **Nick Mohammed Presents The Very Best & Worst of Mr Swallow (Duke of York's); Tiny Echoes, The Missing Light, At The End Of Everything Else, Something Very Far Away (Make Mend And Do European & International Tours).**

As show CSM, theatre includes: **Blues In The Night, Passover (Kiln); Oil (Almeida).**

Julia was the Stage Manager for Richard Alston Dance Company (UK, EU & International Tours) from 2003-2008.

Aneesha Srinivasan
(Assistant Director)

For the Royal Court: **Imposter 22, Word-Play.**

As director, theatre includes: **Brown Girls Do It Too [co-director] (& UK tour), Before I Was A Bear (& Bunker) (Soho); The Woman In the Film (Roundhouse).**

As assistant director, theatre includes: **Name, Place, Animal, Thing (Almeida).**

Julia Wilkens
(Stage Manager Work Placement)

Theatre includes: **Purgatory in Ingolstadt (Embassy); After the Fall (Webber Douglas); Metamorphoses (& Leicester Curve), Hamlet (Courtyard).**

Julia is a current student at the Royal Central School of Speech and Drama.

Fenella Woolgar
(Agrippina Bungay)

For the Royal Court: **Circle Mirror Transformation, Motortown.**

Theatre includes: **Slaves of Solitude (Hampstead); Welcome Home Captain Fox (Donmar); Handbagged (Kiln/West End); Hedda Gabler, The Real Thing (Old Vic); The Veil, Time and the Conways (National); Bronte, Passage to India (Shared Experience); A Midsummer Night's Dream, As You Like It, Bring Me Sunshine (Manchester Royal Exchange); Way Upstream (Derby Playhouse); How the Other Half Loves (Watford Palace); The Miser (Salisbury Playhouse); Charley's Aunt (Sheffield Crucible); The Cherry Orchard (York Theatre Royal).**

Television includes: **The Buccaneers, The Reckoning, Dalgliesh, Call the Midwife, House Party – Unprecedented, Plebs, Midsomer Murders, Quacks, Harlots, Inside No. 9, Home Fires, War and Peace, Spies of Warsaw, Case Histories, Silk, Halloween Party, Poirot, Freezing, Doctor Who, Jekyll, Mr Loveday's Little Outing, He Knew He Was Right, Eroica, The Way We Live Now, People Like Us.**

Film includes: **Mr Jones, Judy, Victoria & Abdul, Whisky Galore, Swallows and Amazons, Mr Turner, Cheerful Weather for the Wedding, You Will Meet a Tall Dark Stranger, St Trinian's, Scoop 2005, Wah Wah, Vera Drake, Stage Beauty, Bright Young Things.**

Awards include: **Clarence Derwent Award (Hedda Gabler).**

Bret Yount (Fight Director)

For the Royal Court: **Imposter 22, Hope has a Happy Meal, Cyprus Avenue (& Abbey, Dublin/Public, NYC), The Cane, Linda, Violence & Son, The Low Road, In Basildon, Wastwater, No Quarter, Belong, Remembrance Day, Redbud, Spur of the Moment, The Nether (& West End).**

Other theatre includes: **The Crucible, Blues for An Alabama Sky, The Middle, Jack Absolute Flies Again, Top Girls, Nine Night, Ma Rainey's Black Bottom, Treasure Island, A Taste of Honey, Emil & the Detectives, The World of Extreme Happiness, Double Feature, Moon on a Rainbow Shawl, Men Should Weep (National); A Little Life, Dirty Dancing, Girl from the North Country (& Old Vic), City of Angels, Caroline or Change, Foxfinder, Red Velvet, The Winter's Tale/Harlequinade, American Buffalo, Bad Jews, Fences, Posh, Absent Friends, Death & the Maiden, Clybourne Park, The Harder They Come, The Lover/The Collection (West End); Richard III, Private Lives (UK tour); Waiting for Godot, Romeo & Juliet, The Effect (Crucible, Sheffield); The Winter's Tale (Cheek by Jowl); A Very Expensive Poison, The Hairy Ape (Old Vic); Nine Night, The Wasp (Trafalgar Studios); The One, Blueberry Toast, First Love is the Revolution (Soho); Hamlet (Barbican); Macbeth, Richard II, The Tempest, Much Ado About Nothing, Romeo & Juliet, Anne Boleyn (Globe); Medea (Gate); Tipping the Velvet (Lyric, Hammersmith); The Pirates of Penzance, La Traviata, The Mastersingers of Nuremberg, La Fanciulla, Benvenuto Cellini, Rodelinda (ENO); King Lear, The Merchant of Venice, Arden of Faversham, The Roaring Girl, Wolf Hall/Bring Up the Bodies, Candide (RSC); 'Tis Pity She's a Whore, The Broken Heart (Sam Wanamaker Playhouse); Force Majeure, Teenage Dick, Europe, Appropriate, Splendour, Roots, City of Angels, The Physicists, The Recruiting Officer (Donmar); All My Sons, Cannibals, Orpheus Descending (Royal Exchange, Manchester); The Trial, A Streetcar Named Desire, A Season in the Congo, Public Enemy (Young Vic); Ghosts (& Trafalgar Studios/BAM, NYC), Chimerica (& West End), Children's Children, The Knot of the Heart, House of Games, Ruined (Almeida); The Norman Conquests, A Streetcar Named Desire, Macbeth, The Caretaker, Lost Monsters (Liverpool Playhouse/Everyman, Liverpool); Village Idiots, After the End, Dangerous Lady, Shalom, Baby, A Clockwork Orange – The Musical, The Graft, Two Women, Gladiator Games, Bashment (Theatre Royal, Stratford East).**

Television includes: **Quick Cuts, Against All Odds, Blue Peter.**

Film includes: **Troy.**

THE ROYAL COURT THEATRE

The Royal Court Theatre is the writers' theatre. It is a leading force in world theatre for cultivating and supporting writers – undiscovered, emerging and established.

Through the writers, the Royal Court is at the forefront of creating restless, alert, provocative theatre about now. We open our doors to the unheard voices and free thinkers that, through their writing, change our way of seeing.

Over 120,000 people visit the Royal Court in Sloane Square, London, each year and many thousands more see our work elsewhere through transfers to the West End and New York, UK and international tours, digital platforms, our residencies across London, and our site-specific work. Through all our work we strive to inspire audiences and influence future writers with radical thinking and provocative discussion.

The Royal Court's extensive development activity encompasses a diverse range of writers and artists and includes an ongoing programme of writers' attachments, readings, workshops and playwriting groups. Twenty years of the International Department's pioneering work around the world means the Royal Court has relationships with writers on every continent.

Since 1956 we have commissioned and produced hundreds of writers, from John Osborne to Jasmine Lee-Jones. Royal Court plays from every decade are now performed on stage and taught in classrooms and universities across the globe.

We strive to create an environment in which differing voices and opinions can co-exist. In current times, it is becoming increasingly difficult for writers to write what they want or need to write without fear, and we will do everything we can to rise above a narrowing of viewpoints.

It is because of this commitment to the writer and our future that we believe there is no more important theatre in the world than the Royal Court.

🐦 royalcourt ⬛ royalcourttheatre

 Supported using public funding by
ARTS COUNCIL ENGLAND

ROYAL

ASSISTED PERFORMANCES

Captioned Performances

Captioned performances are accessible for people who are D/deaf, deafened & hard of hearing, as well as being suitable for people for whom English is not a first language.

Mates in Chelsea
Wednesday 6th December, 7:30pm
Thursday 7th December, 2:30pm

BSL-interpreted Performances

BSL-interpreted performances, delivered by an interpreter, give a sign inteprretation of the text spoken and/or sung by artists in the onstage production.

Mates in Chelsea
Saturday 2nd December, 2:30pm

COURT

ROYAL

ASSISTED PERFORMANCES

Performances in a Relaxed Environment

Relaxed Environment performances are suitable for those who may benefit from a more relaxed environment.

During these performances:
- There is a relaxed attitude to noise in the auditorium; you are welcome to respond to the show in whatever way feels natural
- You can enter and exit the auditorium when needed
- We will help you find the best seats for your experience
- House lights may remain raised slightly
- Loud noises may be reduced

Mates in Chelsea
Saturday 9th December, 2:30pm

If you would like to talk to us about your access requirements, please contact our Box Office at (0)20 7565 5000 or boxoffice@royalcourttheatre.com

The Royal Court Visual Story is available on our website. Story and Sensory synposes are available on the show pages via the Whats On tab of the website shortly after Press Night.

COURT

ROYAL COURT SUPPORTERS

Our incredible community of supporters makes it possible for us to achieve our mission of nurturing and platforming writers at every stage of their careers. Our supporters are part of our essential fabric – they help to give us the freedom to take bigger and bolder risks in our work, develop and empower new voices, and create world-class theatre that challenges and disrupts the theatre ecology.

To all our supporters, thank you. You help us to write the future.

PUBLIC FUNDING

Supported using public funding by
ARTS COUNCIL ENGLAND

CHARITABLE PARTNERS

BackstageTrust

JERWOOD ARTS

CORPORATE SPONSORS

Aqua Financial Ltd
Cadogan
Edwardian Hotels, London
Sustainable Wine Solutions
Walpole

SIS TER

CORPORATE MEMBERS

Bloomberg Philanthopies
Cream
Sloane Stanley

TRUSTS AND FOUNDATIONS

Martin Bowley Charitable Trust
The Noël Coward Foundation
Cowley Charitable Foundation
The D'Oyly Carte Charitable Trust
The Lynne Gagliano Writer's Award
The Golden Bottle Trust
The Harold Hyam Wingate Foundation
John Lyon's Charity
Clare McIntyre's Bursary
Old Possum's Practical Trust
The Austin and Hope Pilkington Trust
Richard Radcliffe Charitable Trust
Rose Foundation
Royal Victoria Hall Foundation
John Thaw Foundation
The Victoria Wood Foundation

ROYAL

BAR & KITCHEN

The Royal Court's Bar & Kitchen aims to create a welcoming and inspiring environment with a style and ethos that reflects the work we put on stage.

Offering expertly crafted cocktails alongside an extensive selection of craft gins and beers, wine and soft drinks, our vibrant basement bar provides a sanctuary in the middle of Sloane Square. By day a perfect spot for meetings or quiet reflection and by night atmospheric meeting spaces for cast, crew, audiences and the general public.

All profits go directly to supporting the work of the Royal Court theatre, cultivating and supporting writers – undiscovered, emerging and established.

For more information, visit
royalcourttheatre.com/bar

HIRES & EVENTS

The Royal Court is available to hire for celebrations, rehearsals, meetings, filming, ceremonies and much more. Our two theatre spaces can be hired for conferences and showcases, and the building is a unique venue for bespoke events and receptions.

For more information, visit
royalcourttheatre.com/events

Sloane Square London, SW1W 8AS ⊖ Sloane Square ⇌ Victoria Station
🐦 royalcourt f theroyalcourttheatre ◎ royalcourttheatre

COURT

Let's be friends. With benefits.

Our Friends and Good Friends are part of the fabric of the Royal Court. They help us to create world-class theatre, and in return they receive early access to our shows and a range of exclusive benefits.

Join today and become a part of our community.

Become a Friend (from £40 a year)

Benefits include:
- Priority Booking
- Advanced access to £12 Monday tickets
- 10% discount in our Bar & Kitchen (including Court in the Square) and Samuel French bookshop

Become a Good Friend (from £95 a year)

In addition to the Friend benefits, our Good Friends also receive:
- Five complimentary playtexts for Royal Court productions
- An invitation for two to step behind the scenes of the Royal Court Theatre at a special annual event

Our Good Friends' membership also includes a voluntary donation. This extra support goes directly towards supporting our work and future, both on and off stage.

To become a Friend or a Good Friend, or to find out more about the different ways in which you can get involved, visit our website: royalcourttheatre.com/support-us

The English Stage Company at the Royal Court Theatre is a registered charity (No. 231242)

Mates in Chelsea

ubi solitudinem faciunt, pacem appellant.
(where they make a desert, they call it peace.)

Tacitus, Agricola XXX

Cast of characters

Tug Bungay
Mrs Hanratty
Charlton Thrupp
Agrippina Bungay
Finty Crossbell
Simone Montesquieu
Oleg Mikhailovich Govorov
Two Assassins

Settings

I – *Tug Bungay's flat, Chelsea, London; a summer's day*

II – *Dimley Grange castle, Northumberland; the next afternoon*

III – *The smouldering wreckage thereof; a short while later*

Time

The present

Act One

A bright early summer's afternoon in the opulently furnished flat of Theodore 'Tug' Bungay in Chelsea, London. Mrs Hanratty, the housekeeper, is sharpening a cake slice while singing the Soviet national anthem. Tug enters, nonchalantly.

Tug Sharpening a cake slice while singing the Soviet national anthem again, are we, Mrs Hanratty?

Mrs Hanratty One must always be primed for the moment of insurrectionary violence, Theodore.

Tug Well, I just hope that when the revolution comes it changes as little as possible.

Mrs Hanratty I wouldn't worry too much, sir. This is England, after all. But I live in optimistic readiness.

Tug Speaking of social upheaval, is everything prepared for my mother's visit?

Mrs Hanratty Yes, the Victoria Sponge is cooling plump and pillow-like on the sideboard, the bedroom's been aired, the sinks have been wiped, and the toilet seat has been returned to its preferred downward configuration.

Tug I appreciate it, Mrs Hanratty. Mothers can be viciously particular.

Mrs Hanratty They can when you piss on the carpet, sir. There was also a message from Miss Crossbell.

Tug Finty! What does it say?

Mrs Hanratty (*reading*) 'To the Right Honourable the Viscount Bungay, Cadogan Square, London, SW–

Tug No need to read the address, just tell me what it says! Does she forgive me?

Mrs Hanratty 'Dear Tuggy, I greatly enjoyed the vast bouquet of apologetically seasonal flowers, but in response to the accompanying missive, I would ask that you take that small, pink, peeled-prawn-looking thing which you so generously dub a manhood and kindly go and fuck yourself.'

Tug   I'll take that as a no, then. Oh, Finty! She may despise me, but she writes a beautiful letter.

Mrs Hanratty   Shall I send anything in reply?

Tug   More flowers. And biscuits. And say something nice about her appearance or something, that might work.

Mrs Hanratty   Good to see romance isn't dead. (*Making to go*.) Right, well, barring the overthrow of the nation state, then, I'll be in the kitchen inventing compliments about your fiancée's hair.

Tug   You know, I've often wondered if it doesn't in some small way contradict your Leninist principles to have a job wiping sinks for a viscount, Mrs Hanratty?

Mrs Hanratty   Not in this economy, sir. I'll bring the tea through in a minute.

The doorbell rings.

Tug   Actually, you'd better answer that first.

Mrs Hanratty *nods and goes to answer the door.*

Tug   Oh God, I hope that's not my mother already. The last thing I need is for her to have learned to be punctual. People being on time is so exhausting.

Mrs Hanratty *returns.*

Mrs Hanratty   Mr Charlton Thrupp.

Charlie Thrupp *appears, dressed as an Afghan tribesman.* **Mrs Hanratty** *goes out.*

Tug   Charlie? Oh, Charlie, it's so good to see you! I almost didn't recognise you there for a moment! Where was it this time? India?

Charlie   Close but no hashish-pipe, my friend. (*Heroically.*) Afghanistan.

He drops his luggage theatrically to the floor.

Tug   Goodness, Charlie. Not the dangerous bit, I hope.

Charlie   It's Afghanistan, Tug. It's all the dangerous bit. Particularly now our noble countrymen have hightailed it for good. It's lost none of its 'rustic charm', though. Good food. Lovely people. (*Looking longingly at* **Tug**.) A perfect haven from the heartbreak of London.

Tug (*oblivious*)   Sounds splendid.

Charlie   Yes, there's nothing that remedies a romantic affliction like a stint in Central Asia, land of The Great Game.

Tug   What, rugby?

Charlie   No, the intricate acts of diplomatic subterfuge whereby the British and Russian Empires exploited for their own gain the complex web of interdependent Afghan tribal allegiances during the nineteenth century with geopolitical repercussions reverberating even to this day. It was fascinating to see its fallout on the ground. I walked across the whole country don't you know?

Tug   Impressive.

Charlie   Only at the very narrowest part, mind. Took well over an hour, though. I was knackered!

Tug   That does sound rather dangerous, Charlie. Don't you stick out like a sore thumb as you toddle between the villages?

Charlie   Oh, hardly. I blend right in. (*Twirling in his costume.*) Observe my authentic couture, my friend! You really think I'd go on a jaunt like that without first dressing for the role? Don't be ridiculous. I have a chap who makes these outfits for me. The finest Cultural Stylist in all of London! There you are, take a look at that.

He hands **Tug** *a business card.*

Charlie   Nothing but complete transformation! Total assimilation! I always pay him a visit wherever I'm off to, be it the souks of the Middle East or the secret military compounds of Latin America. I've even been known to pop by before heading out to some of the less hospitable parts of Hertfordshire. If you ever need to look the part, just give him a call.

Tug (*pocketing the card*)   Thanks.

Charlie   Of course, when it comes to Afghanistan, it helps that I speak all forty-three of various tribal dialects fluently.

Tug   Fluently?

Charlie   Fluently.

Tug   Fluently?

Charlie   Fluently.

Tug   Fluently?

Charlie   *Fluente.*

Tug   *Fluenti.*

Charlie   *Completamente fluento.* So I can charm my way out of a potential hostage situation wherever I happen to be.

Tug   I prefer my holidays a little more sedate.

Charlie   Oh, where's your spirit of adventure, Tuggy? Besides, it's not as if I'm ever in any actual danger. One of the great benefits of possessing a stupendous amount of wealth and privilege is I can do pretty much anything with precisely zero consequences.

Tug   Except for the increasingly unstable political situation in the region.

Charlie   Oh, you are funny, Tuggy! I meant zero consequences *for me*. Perhaps a few fragile alliances get fractured or a few priceless artefacts end up in the wrong person's wheelie-case, but no harm no foul in the long run. And if I ever make eyes at the wrong warlord's nephew, I just hop on the satellite phone, give the boys in the RAF a quick buzz and before you know it a Chinook swoops in to literally airlift me out of the situation. Not bad, eh?

Tug   Not bad at all. I'll give you a call if I ever need a helicopter, then.

Charlie   Do. Listen, viscount, you don't mind if I spark up a bit of opium, do you? I've developed quite an itch for the stuff.

Tug   Under normal circumstances I'd say yes. Under normal circumstances I'd be joining you. But, unfortunately, my mother's about to materialise and I don't think she'd react too fondly if she arrived to find you lolling stupefied on the divan like a disgraced Victorian detective.

Charlie   Ah, the gorgon of Dimley Grange castle swoops down from the north! Not in financial trouble, are we?

Tug   No, the funds are in rude fettle, I'm assured. Mother and the money-folk are on excellent terms. She even plays daily badminton matches with her account manager.

Charlie   Right. So, why's the dowager descending, then?

Tug   Oh, just her customary biannual visit: so it'll be the standard dressing down for my extravagant spending, at which point I'll don the old sack cloth and ashes, say 'I'm very sorry, mummy' a few times, and then she'll pootle off back to Northumberland irked but temporarily placated.

Mrs Hanratty *enters.*

Mrs Hanratty   A response from Miss Crossbell, sir.

Tug (*eagerly*)   Yes?

Mrs Hanratty (*reading*)   'Dear Tuggy, although I continue to appreciate the apologetically seasonal flowers, and the beautiful biscuits, along with the exquisitely rhymed sonnet cycle in praise of my tresses in the moonlight –' (*Looks at* **Tug**.) You're welcome, by the way. (*Back to reading*.) 'I still refuse to accept your apology and still insist you take your miniscule and peeled-prawn-like –

Tug   Okay, I think we've had enough now, Mrs Hanratty –

Mrs Hanratty (*reading*)   'Take your miniscule and peeled-prawn-like manhood –

Tug   Mrs Hanratty! Stop!

Mrs Hanratty (*reading*)   'And fuck yourself in your overeducated, underemployed, titled twat face. Signed, Finty Crossbell.'

Tug (*sheepishly*)   Good. Good stuff.

Mrs Hanratty   Shall I send anything else?

Tug   Biscuits. More biscuits.

Mrs Hanratty   All right, then. (*To* **Charlie**.) And anything for yourself, there, Mr Thrupp? Hookah pipe? An audition for an insensitive production of Aladdin?

Charlie   I'm good, thanks, Mrs H.

Mrs Hanratty   Right you are.

Mrs Hanratty *goes.*

Charlie   Finty really does write a lovely letter.

Tug   She really does. A lovely letter.

Charlie   What have you done this time, Tug?

Tug   Well, the height of summer's fast approaching, so I've decided, as any sensible person would, to spend the next two months at my castle, drinking and fishing, and shooting, and drinking, and thinking, and walking, and also drinking. Alone. Figuratively speaking.

Charlie   Figuratively speaking?

Tug   Well, without Finty, at any rate.

Charlie   And you can see how that might annoy her, can't you?

Tug   Of course I can see how that might annoy her! But she wouldn't want to come even if I asked her. The woman thinks the countryside's full of badly dressed animal-murderers. She's never donned a welly in her life. Look, I'm very fond of Finty. She's attractive and kind and she has great hair and above average teeth and runs the finest online-only lifestyle magazine in south-west London. I'm proud and honoured to call her my fiancée. I just wish I didn't have to, you know, see her or talk to her, ever.

Charlie (*placing his hand over* **Tug***'s*)   It sounds like your heart's not really in this, my friend.

Tug   But I can't exactly break up with her, can I?

Charlie   Why not?

Tug   Because we've been engaged for seven years! That's longer than most people's mortgages!

Charlie   It really isn't.

Tug   Well, I don't know anything about mortgages, do I? It's a long time, is my point. Not marrying her after this long would just be embarrassing. Plus, on a mercenary note, she's the heiress to the Crossbell haulage empire, so if the funds ever dry up, she can maintain me in the manner to which I've become accustomed.

Charlie (*tenderly*)   If you're ever feeling hard up, my friend, you know you could always ask me.

Tug   I've got it! Why don't you come with me to Dimley Grange, Charlie? Finty desperately disapproves of all the cheese-guzzling and claret-swilling I'd be doing up there on my own, but if I were cheese-guzzling and claret-swilling with you she'd be bound to think better of the endeavour.

Charlie   I didn't realise she held me in such high regard.

Tug   Oh, she doesn't, Charlie, she hates you, she thinks you're an arrogant snake, an irritating neo-colonial blowhard, but the word is you're pegged for high office one day, so she's determined that I keep in with you anyway. So what do you say?

Charlie (*shy*)   Erm, well I'm flattered, obviously, but I, erm, don't know if I could stand to be for so long in such close proximity to . . . (*Pulling himself together.*) What I mean is, the Kazakhs are testing a new commercial space shuttle and I've heard there's a spare slot on the passenger roster.

Tug   Oh, bugger the Kazakhs, Charlie! Dimley Grange is my joy. You'd have the most wonderful time there. It's the best place in the world! The sound of the sea wakes you up in the morning, the light has that fragile, far-northern quality, and in the evening, when the last sun glints bittersweetly over the battlements and you feel the breeze on your face, an almost ecumenical quiet descends like delicate cloud and you'd never wish to be anywhere else but England. It's the closest thing I've ever known to peace. I do wish you'd come with me, Charlie. I wish I could see that with you.

Charlie (*moved*)   Well, there is a fairly high chance of a launch disaster. And I have been hitting the old opium pipe a little hard lately. So maybe it's time to bash it into a ploughshare and settle down for a quiet life in the country. I'm in, mate.

Tug   Fantastic.

Charlie   You know, I can almost see us now, bustling about the place in matching Barbour jackets, pointing at things with big sticks and releasing the occasional mountain lion back into the ecosystem, then cosying up by the fireside at night, you sipping a fine single malt in a wingback chair and me at the desk, penning vol. one of my memoirs.

Tug   Sounds heavenly.

The doorbell.

(*Nervous.*) Or it might be worth calling the Kazakhs after all.
I could do with being blasted off into orbit right about now.

Charlie   No, now you must stand and face your demons,
Tuggy. Or gorgons, as the case may be.

Tug   Do I have to?

Charlie   We can do it together.

Mrs Hanratty *enters.*

Mrs Hanratty   The Viscountess, Agrippina, Lady Bung –

Agrippina Bungay *steams in.*

Agrippina   No need for the frippery, Mrs Hanratty. I can
make my presence felt by being present. (**Mrs Hanratty** *goes.*
Agrippina *notices* **Charlie**.) Oh, you're here, Charlie. I
almost didn't recognise you there for a moment. You look
like an idiot.

Charlie   Nice to see you too, Lady Bungay.

Agrippina   Theodore, you look fat.

Tug   Thank you, mother.

Agrippina   I didn't intend that as a compliment.

Tug   I didn't take it as one.

A steely silence.

Charlie   Right, I'd best be heading off, then.

Agrippina   Oh, no, do stay, Charlie. We're sadly devoid of
such outlandishly dressed persons in my remote part of the
North East. You're a treat for my tired eyes.

Tug   Why don't you sit down, mother? It must've been an
arduous journey.

Mrs Hanratty *returns with tea and cake and begins to distribute it.*

Agrippina   It always is on this country's so-called 'rail network'. But thank you, I will. (*Sits.*) You, on the other hand, Theodore, had best remain standing. I find the sight of a seated man somewhat disturbing. It's unnatural, somehow. Your late father despised sitting down. He saw it as a sign of weakness. Though it did become, by the end, rather inconvenient, for meals and the like. He even died standing up, which took no small amount of concentration. But, he was principled to the last, your father, and I loved him for that, Theodore.

Tug   Mother, how many times have I told you not to call me Theodore? Only dentists, cold callers and Mrs Hanratty refer to me by my Christian name. Just call me Tug like everyone else does.

Agrippina   I refuse to employ that revolting appellation. (*Shuddering.*) 'Tug.' The very sound of it conjures dark whiffs of the lost property bin in a boys' boarding school changing room. Do you not hate it too, Charlie?

Tug   Don't ask him, he's the one who came up with it in the first place.

Agrippina (*to* **Charlie**)   So I have you to blame for the ignominy of my son being referred to as a transitive verb?

Charlie   My apologies, Lady Bungay. The name felt so apt that it almost invented itself.

Agrippina (*to* **Tug**)   Well, you're my son, and until I think of you as otherwise, I will refer to you by the name I gave you: Theodore, after my dear beloved Roosevelt. Though unlike that presidential titan you seem to possess no talent for innovation when it comes to economic policy.

Tug   Are you referring to my finances, mother?

Agrippina   I am, or lack thereof, I ought to say. A record of your recent monthly outgoings reads like the shopping list for an oil baron's birthday party. (*Takes out a long bank statement and looks at it.*) Here we are: caviar, oysters, lobster: you spend more in a month on fresh seafood than some small inland economies do in a year! Champagne, expensive whisky. The largest floristry bill since the Dutch tulip bubble. What on earth are you doing buying so many flowers?

Tug   I'm forced to make a lot of apologies, okay?

Agrippina   Well, the next time you find yourself in desperate need of absolution, why don't you think of your savings account and try, I don't know, saying some words and meaning them, instead?

Tug   Oh, don't be ridiculous, mother. Nobody does that these days. Charlie, you'll back me up on this, won't you?

Charlie   He's right, Lady Bungay. I try my best not to mean anything, wherever possible. It's really the simplest way.

Agrippina   What a hopelessly vacuous sentiment.

Charlie (*pleased*)   Aww, thank you, Lady Bungay.

Agrippina (*to* **Tug**)   Well, you may be content to persist in a fug of happy nihilism but your bank balance won't be. Let me put this in terms even you'll understand: if you continue to spend at this rate, it will only continue to go down. And with no income or job to speak of, you have no means of making it go up.

Tug (*disgusted*)   Ugh, 'job'. Such a vulgar word.

Agrippina   Yes, Theodore. A job. An employment. Like a banker or a politician or whatever it is Charlie does for a living.

Charlie   Adventurer cum wandering scholar cum author cum deejay cum international politics podcast host.

Agrippina   Precisely.

Tug   But I do have a job. I'm a professional viscount.

Agrippina   The title alone isn't enough these days, Theodore. You need to leverage your position into something lucrative. There are plenty of things you could do, in my opinion. Start a charity by pretending to care about the environment? Open a finishing school for the children of rich foreign businessmen? Star, alongside your friends, in a light-hearted reality TV show about your various London-based hijinks?

Tug *and* **Charlie** *look at each other for a moment.*

Tug   No.

Charlie   God, no.

Tug   Absolutely not!

Charlie   Terrible idea!

Agrippina   I'm just telling you times have changed. Being an aristocrat isn't something you do anymore, Theodore, it's just something you are.

Tug   Exactly. I see it as a kind of calling. A vocation, if you will. And I do do things. I shoot, I fish, I have lunch.

Agrippina   Having lunch is not a vocation.

Tug   That depends on the lunch.

Agrippina   Well, you may have to go hungry shortly. Because there's hardly any cash left.

Tug   What are you talking about? The funds are in rude fettle, you've always assured me. What happened to playing badminton with your account manager?

Agrippina   My aiding Simone with her drop strokes has no relevance to this conversation.

Tug   So where's it all gone, then? What have you been spending it on? Ordering an endless supply of shuttlecocks? Making gigantic contributions to the Conservative Party?

Agrippina   I don't donate to left-wing pressure groups. I'm appalled that you'd even suggest that. Until they start paying attention to the real people of this country, they're not getting a penny from me.

Mrs Hanratty   Can't help but agree with you on that one, Lady Bungay.

Agrippina   Thank you, Mrs Hanratty.

Tug   Then where's it all gone?

Agrippina   You haven't been listening to me at all! You spent it, you moron! On your seafood and your flowers and your bizarre-looking trousers and this mortgaged-up-to-the-eyeballs Chelsea pied-à-terre staffed by your wise-cracking housekeeper, like you're some sort of depressed elderly clergyman! You're thirty years old, Theodore! You're perfectly capable of taking your own messages!

Mrs Hanratty   Oh, that reminds me, sir, there was another message from Miss Crossbell.

Tug   Probably not the time, Mrs Hanratty.

Agrippina   Announcing your guests into your apartment like they're characters in a Henry James novel.

Tug   It makes me feel special.

Agrippina   And it makes them feel like competitors at Crufts! There is no need for this woman to be here, she is a worthless parasite and your continued employment of her is an obscene and ridiculous profligacy. (*To* **Mrs Hanratty**.) The cake is delicious, by the way, Mrs Hanratty.

Mrs Hanratty   Thank you, Lady Bungay. It's technically a Victoria, this one, but I refuse to give it a monarchist name, so I've dubbed it 'The People's Sponge'.

Agrippina   How very democratic of you. And, tell me, which of your comrades in the local proletariat bank-rolls these experiments in egalitarian baking?

Tug   Mother, I won't have you disparaging Mrs Hanratty like this. She's been with me since Oxford.

Charlie   And she's a legend. She was the only member of the college bedmaking staff brave enough to deal with what he did to his rooms after formal dinner.

Mrs Hanratty   Indeed, Lady Bungay. I saw unspeakable things.

Tug   And besides, this is a mutual arrangement. Given Mrs Hanratty's rather chequered CV, no one else would hire her. With the job market the way it is at the moment, I'm the only thing standing between her and the Deliveroo.

Mrs Hanratty   And I couldn't be a Deliveroo, Lady Bungay. Not in this skirt.

Agrippina   Your skirt is immaterial here.

Mrs Hanratty   Actually, it's quite a nice polyester.

Tug   Mother, you seem to be forgetting that I am a gentleman. And a gentleman doesn't do anything he can pay someone else to do for him.

Agrippina   Yes, but you can't afford to pay those people anymore because you have no money! When will you get it through your thick and childish skull?! The money is gone! It's gone, gone, gone! And gone because you spent it all!

Silence.

Tug (*hangdog*)   I'm very sorry, Mummy.

Agrippina   Your meaningless apologies will have no truck with me this time.

Tug   I'll try and be a bit more meaningful, then. Wait a minute. (*Looks even more hangdog.*) I'm very sorry, mummy. (*Checking himself.*) No, no, that wasn't quite right, I'll try again, I can mean it, I can mean it. (*Looks even more hangdog.*) I'm very sorry, mummy.

Agrippina   Theodore. Does the name Oleg Mikhailovich Govorov mean anything to you?

Tug   Yes, he's the chap in *Crime and Punishment*, isn't he? Not the main guy, the sort of villain character.

Agrippina   No.

Tug   Oh, no, that's right, he's the fellow from *War and Peace*. Again, not the main guy –

Agrippina   No, he's not a character of literary invention. He's very much a Russian of the flesh and blood variety.

Charlie   He's an oligarch, right?

Agrippina   Very good, Charlie. He's an oligarch.

Tug   Oh. One of the good ones or one of the bad ones?

Agrippina   I wasn't aware we made moral distinctions when it comes to that particular class of individual.

Tug   You know, like, is he one of the billionaire, tax-avoiding, ethnonationalist, former-KGB-now-British-tabloid-owning oligarchs, or one of the bad ones?

Agrippina   In that case, very much one of the good ones. Indeed, some might say he's *the* oligarch. He amassed his vast fortune in 1990s Saint Petersburg, taking out bank loans to buy privatisation vouchers, and using them to purchase former state assets on the cheap: gas plants, automobile factories, ice hockey teams, that sort of thing. A display of pecuniary get-up-and-go of which you, Theodore, could only dream. Unfortunately, things turned sour for him when one of his several television channels broadcast a satirical variety show which at one point made oblique reference to the rather diminutive stature of the current president, an insult which that grumpy and frankly rather humourless fascist didn't take too kindly. Govorov became *persona non grata* after that and disappeared from Russia, and, indeed, the public view entirely, lest he run up against the wrong end of a poisoned perfume dispenser or radioactive teapot.

Thus, he's been off the map completely for the last twenty years, surfacing only occasionally for a do on one of the world's more discreet superyachts or briefly bobbing up in the Cayman Islands to turn the money over. He's not been photographed once, all that time. No one even knows what he looks like now. And he's never returned to the Motherland. Must be sad, for such a patriot.

Mrs Hanratty (*collecting up the plates*)   A Russian, is he? I wonder if he knows Vladimir Ilych.

Agrippina   I'm sure he knows a whole host of Vladimirs, Mrs Hanratty.

Tug   She's referring specifically to Lenin, mother. So no, Mrs Hanratty, however wide his social circle I doubt it extends to dictators who died nearly a century ago.

Mrs Hanratty (*leaving*)   Well you never know, do you, Theodore? You never know.

She goes out.

Tug   In this precise case, I think I do. But what's this Govorov got to do with me and my money?

Agrippina   Well, I was recently contacted by one of Mr Govorov's personal representatives. It seems sanctions arising from the war in Ukraine are making his multinational lifestyle rather difficult, so he plans to settle down in one place. He's alighted on England, due to its temperate climate and welcoming attitude towards money laundering. He found Dimley Grange on the internet and apparently has fallen rather in love.

Tug   What? You mean he wants to buy the castle?

Agrippina   He doesn't just want to, he's going to. He's made an exorbitant offer, far above the going market price, and in cash, no less. So that's that, as far as I'm concerned.

Tug   But why Dimley Grange? Can't he buy somewhere else? He's supposedly one of the world's richest Russians, and Dimley Grange isn't even the nicest castle in Northumberland.

Agrippina   No, but it is the most remote. It's by some distance the furthest from any of the North East's already pitiful selection of main roads and transport links. It has a protected clifftop location, is situated in a signal black hole, and maintains a strange resistance to the installation of wi-fi routers. It is, quite literally, a fortress, and as such is perfect for a safety-conscious Russian dissident.

Tug   But he can't just pitch up and buy the castle! It's a piece of our family! A piece of history! The then-future Charles the Second once stayed there when he was on the run from the Roundheads!

Agrippina   Oh, that doesn't make it anything special, Theodore. The then-future Charles the Second stayed everywhere when he was on the run from the Roundheads. That man would've stayed in a horse-trough, as long as it furnished him with a pint and a nice piece of fanny.

Tug   So I just say goodbye to my birth-right, do I? To the place where I grew up?

Agrippina   I warned you it might come to this, Theodore. I told you again and again. But you refused my plans to lease out the Great Hall, or convert any of the barns and outbuildings, and you pointed a shotgun at the nice lady from the National Trust!

Tug   I'd hasten to remind you, mother, that this particular Englishman's castle is his home!

Agrippina   Allow me to tell you a story, Theodore. Once upon a time, almost a full millennium ago, your ancestor, one Thaddeus Aloysius de Bungaie, a truculent blacksmith from the Rouen region, arrived on these shores with William the Conqueror. Having distinguished himself at Hastings, the freshly-crowned King Will tasked young Thad with deploying his talent for violence to subdue the marauding

Vikings and woad-painted natives of the far northern reaches of his new kingdom. Thaddeus achieved this goal with considerable success, for which the king ennobled him and provided him with a fortune and land, upon which he set a modest castle, Le Grange du Dimlie, named for the small barn he burned down to build it. As the steady centuries rolled by, the fortune gradually diminished, until it reached you, who appear have spent what little remains of it on smoked salmon. The game is up and all that's left is the castle. Which many would say you never deserved in the first place. You know, much like a lot of the very rich people in this country, you didn't earn your wealth through hard work or talent or sudden commercial inspiration or even, like I did, through a calculating upward marriage, but through the thievery and violence of one of your distant relations.

Tug   You ought to be careful, Lady Bungay. You're starting to speak like a socialist.

Agrippina   Don't use foul language in front of your mother, Theodore. I merely state the plain and simple truth. You've only been able to carry on as you have because your thirty times great grandfather was peculiarly good at punching people. You've got where you are through sheer stupid luck and it's amazing you've even got this far. It's time to take the money and go.

Tug   But I don't want to take the money and go.

Agrippina   Ludicrous child! This isn't about what you want. You have until tomorrow. For in twenty-four hours, almost precisely, Oleg Mikhailovich Govorov will step out of the shadows to arrive at Dimley Grange and take brief tour, before finalising the sale. I will be there, along with my account manager Simone, who will handle the paperwork. And you will be there, I hope, to add your spider-like signature to the notarised deeds.

Tug   And what if I don't show up?

Agrippina   Then I'll leave you to the mercy of the bailiffs. It's up to you. But you may wish to say goodbye to the old place. I certainly know I will. And I'd appreciate the assistance of Mrs Hanratty, to provide a light buffet-style high tea.

Tug (*cowed*)   I'm sure she'd be capable of that.

Agrippina   Very good, then. Well, I'd better be on my way. I have a late badminton appointment and I'm anxious to make the East Coast Mainline before the clientele start getting too inebriated. Until tomorrow, Theodore! Four p.m. sharp! Tell Mrs Hanratty I'll show myself out. (*As she's leaving, proudly.*) I, at least, am old enough to operate my own door handles.

She goes.

Tug (*agitated*)   Oh, goodness, Charlie, this is outrageous! She can't just sell my castle! What am I going to do?

Charlie   Erm, I've no idea, mate, to be honest.

Tug   This is outrageous!

Charlie   I know.

Tug   No, no, you don't; just think about it from my point of view: how would you feel if someone was selling your castle?

Charlie   I don't have a castle.

Tug   But what if you did, Charlie?! What if you did have a castle and someone was trying to sell it?! How would that make you feel?! Why can't anyone around here just see things from my point of view?!

Charlie   I suppose it would be a great devastation to my sense of self.

Tug (*calming down*)   Thank you, Charlie. That's all I needed to hear. Thank you.

Tug *sits down and puts his head in his hands.*

Charlie   I guess that's our summer plans up the spout, then. Farewell to the bucolic retreat. No more frolicking in nature like a pair of lithesome shepherd-boys.

Tug   It's the whole bloody thing up the spout, Charlie. I don't know who I am without that place.

Mrs Hanratty *returns.*

Mrs Hanratty   Oh, has your mother left already? There was a message just came through for her from the representative of an Oleg Mikhailovich Govorov.

Tug (*looking up*)   What? What does it say?

Mrs Hanratty   Just that Mr Govorov will be unable to attend tomorrow's meeting. There's been some kind of a security issue, apparently.

Tug   A security issue?

Mrs Hanratty   Indeed. You'd have thought the Russians would be far too busy torching Ukrainian villages to chase one of their own across the Northumbrian countryside but there we are. He hopes you can reschedule for another time.

Tug   Oh. Right.

Mrs Hanratty   Shall I send any response?

Tug   Erm. Not just yet, Mrs Hanratty. Thank you.

Mrs Hanratty *goes.*

Charlie   Mate, this is perfect.

Tug   Yes, what a relief! Stand down the firing squad! A stay of execution for old Tuggy!

Charlie   Well, no.

Tug   What do you mean, 'no'?

Charlie   Well, it really doesn't change anything materially in the short term. Chaps like that don't back off so easily.

Tug So?

Charlie So, Govorov's folks get in touch with your mum in a few days' time and the castle still gets sold.

Tug Oh. So why is it perfect, then?

Charlie What?

Tug You just said, 'this is perfect'. What do you suggest I do?

Charlie Well, what do you think I suggest you do?

Tug I don't know. What do you think I think you suggest I do?

Charlie What do you think I think you think I suggest you do?

Tug I don't know or I wouldn't be asking!

Charlie Well, Govorov's not coming to the castle tomorrow. But as far as your mother and her racket-sporting banker friend are aware, he still is.

Tug So?

Charlie So, I pay a visit to my Cultural Stylist and then 'Govorov' can still attend.

Tug Why are you doing 'air quotes'?

Charlie Because I'll be disguised as Govorov.

Tug Don't be ridiculous. What good would that do?

Charlie It wouldn't do any good at all. Quite the opposite, in fact. But that's precisely the point. If we go ahead as things stand, then Govorov simply buys Dimley Grange a little further down the line. But, if I go over there tomorrow as 'Govorov' and completely scupper the sale, just horrifically torpedo the whole thing, then there's no way your mother or the banker lady will desire any future contact with Govorov or his people, the deal never happens in the first place, your beloved home is saved and Charlie Thrupp gets made an OBE for services to friendship!

Tug   But, Charlie, won't they realise you're not Govorov?

Charlie   No! This is just why I said that it's perfect. You heard your mother, didn't you? Govorov's a ghost. He's hardly been seen for the last twenty years. And he certainly hasn't been photographed: make a quick image search of the man and the last thing you get is from 2003. A person can change a lot in that time. He could look like frankly anyone now.

Tug   Okay, I'll grant that the man could look quite different from earlier photos, but I'm still sure my mother will be more than slightly surprised when the middle-aged Russian she's supposed to meet tomorrow turns out to be the precise spitting image of you!

Charlie   So this is where my Stylist comes in. This guy's magnificent. He really is the best in the business. I've made use of his outfits all over the world, wherever I need to blend in. He made me enough of a hunky Australian diving instructor to seduce all the gap-year students. He made me enough of a grizzled Belgian mercenary to get me extradited for war crimes.

Tug   Yes, but anyone who knows you will see it's really you.

Charlie   Really me?

Tug   Yes. Charlton Thrupp. Thirty years old. English. My best friend.

Charlie   Oh, Tuggy, surely you can afford to think a little more fluidly about things? These days as long as you possess the wealth and the privilege there's no limit to who you can pretend to be. Oleg Mikhailovich buys himself a castle, a passport and a new library at Cambridge and suddenly he's as English as damp Yorkshire puddings. Charlie Thrupp pays his Stylist enough cash and now he's the perfect Russian. I'm sure he could even make you a good enough Govorov to convince your mother.

Tug   But how on earth does he do it, practically speaking?

Charlie   I honestly have no idea. Makeup, maybe? Something to do with magnets, perhaps? There's possibly, like, a concealed mirror somewhere? He doesn't reveal his secrets. The point is that it works. So, I can just pop on down to his emporium before it shuts this afternoon, get him to make the necessary adjustments to my Russian oligarch outfit, and then we'll be ready to go!

Tug   You already have a Russian oligarch outfit?

Charlie   Yes, of course I do. You can't get a table in Mayfair these days without claiming to own a Siberian oil field.

Tug   No, Charlie. I won't allow it. Just . . . No.

Charlie   Why on earth not? I'd be perfect. I studied Russian history at college, if you remember, and I've read over six books on the subject, three of which I've written myself, so I think if anyone has the right to impersonate a Russian it's me. I speak the language *completamente fluento*, I have the accent down to a tee, and can even sprinkle in a few choice nuggets of authentic-sounding backstory for extra detail. I was literally born for the role!

Tug   No. No, this is far too serious a situation for so ridiculous a ruse, and you are far too ridiculous a man.

Charlie   Ridiculous?

Tug   I will not entrust the future of my home, of my peace, to someone so reckless, so silly, and who has a marked and frequent tendency to go around ruining everything.

Charlie   But that's exactly what this situation needs! It needs someone to ruin everything!

Tug   Yes, but you're such a dreadful liability that I bet you'd even ruin ruining everything! You can't even order a sandwich without causing a diplomatic incident!

Charlie   I won't be blamed for that. It was a very contentious sandwich.

Tug   Well, you won't get a chance to cause trouble at Dimley Grange because I forbid you to attend.

Charlie   Please! Why won't you listen when I'm trying to help you?

Tug   Because you can't help me here, Charlie! The castle is going to be sold. I just need to accept that and move on.

Charlie   But what about our life in the country?

Tug   It wasn't a life; just a summer.

Charlie (*crestfallen*)   But I'd already picked out a safe rural seat!

Tug (*blowing up a bit*)   Ugh, you always do this! Barrelling in headlong and foolhardy with your overblown schemes! No one is dressing up as an oligarch tomorrow, Charlie, least of all you! You're ridiculous!

Charlie   At least I'm not boring! You're a very boring man, Tug Bungay! Boring!

Finty Crossbell *rushes in suddenly.*

Finty   I couldn't agree more. He's boring, and conceited, and haughty, and dim, and lazy, and selfish, and silly, and vain, and a terrible masseur, and an even worse chef, and he has a manhood which bears more than a passing resemblance to a permanently reticent crustacean.

Mrs Hanratty *rushes in too.*

Mrs Hanratty (*presenting her*)   Miss Finty Crossbell.

Mrs Hanratty *goes.*

Tug   Hello, Finty.

Finty   Good afternoon, Tuggy. And Charlie! Almost didn't recognise you there. A pleasure to see you, as always.

Charlie   Finty! A joy! A delight!

They kiss and break apart.

Finty (*under breath*)   Arrogant snake.

Charlie (*under breath*)   Duplicitous she-tiger.

Finty   Oh, look! Cake! (*She helps herself to a slice.*) Now, Charlie, you'll have to regale us with tales of your latest adventures. I was thinking of writing a profile of you, you know. This might be a good place to start.

Charlie   No, I ought to be going, actually, Finty. I'm feeling a little ridiculous all of a sudden.

Tug   Charlie –

Charlie   It's fine. If your fiancé's not interested in listening to me, Finty, that's fine. If you don't care that I'm the only way to save your castle, Tug, that's absolutely fine by me.

Tug   Charlie, wait –

Charlie (*starting to go*)   No, no. I can see that I'm not wanted here. You know what they say: two's company, three's too much of a challenge to the long-entrenched social norms of monogamy. But it's fine. I suppose I'll ring the Kazakh space program after all. And when my shuttle explodes over the steppe in a million fiery pieces, I'll make sure they post you an earlobe or a foot, to remember me by. Fare you well, Tug Bungay. Farewell forever.

He goes.

Tug   I wasn't expecting you, Finty. If I had, I'd have bought some more flowers.

Finty   Did you not get my last message?

Tug   I've had a pretty busy afternoon, I'm afraid.

Finty   Well, I was quite prepared to give up on you for good, but then Mrs Hanratty managed to tempt me over with the promise of a fresh piece of her delicious sponge. You ought to be thanking your lucky stars for that woman, Tuggy. The number of times her baking skills have saved you from the brink of disaster must be too many to count.

Tug   So you've decided to forgive me, then?

Finty   I wouldn't go that far. But I'm seriously considering the possibility, yes. But first I must insist that you answer this short questionnaire on the current state of our relationship. (*Pulls out a questionnaire and reads it.*) First question: do you love me?

Tug   Define love. I mean, yes.

Finty   Have you ever cheated on me?

Tug   Not knowingly.

Finty   How many times unknowingly?

Tug   Low double figures, I think.

Finty   What's your attitude towards my cheating on you?

Tug   Not on Christmas or my birthday.

Finty   Why, after seven long years of engagement have you still made no headway in arranging our wedding?

Tug   I can't find an available photographer.

Finty   And does your mother still disapprove of our union?

Tug   Yes, she insists I shouldn't wed any lower than an Honourable.

Finty   And remains convinced of that fact?

Tug   She does.

Finty   But you're nevertheless still determined to marry me?

Tug   I am. In due course.

Finty   Good. Congratulations, Tuggy. I forgive you. You may kiss me.

They kiss.

Again.

They kiss again.

I'm satisfied. Oh, Tuggy. Perhaps you are boring, and conceited, and haughty, and dim, and lazy, and selfish, and silly, and vain, and a terrible masseur, and an even worse chef, and you certainly do have a manhood which bears more than a passing resemblance to a permanently reticent crustacean. But I love you all the same. Maybe I'm an idiot.

Tug   Mm, maybe.

Finty   But we're two idiots made for each other. Now, what was all that about with Charlie?

Tug   What was all what?

Finty   'It's the only way to save your castle.'

Tug   Oh, that. Well, my mother's determined to sell Dimley Grange tomorrow, but it's nothing that my good friend Charlie Thrupp can't solve by visiting his Cultural Stylist and arranging to impersonate a Russian oligarch.

Finty   Excuse me?

Tug *takes out the Stylist's business card and shows it to* **Finty**.

Finty   Give me that.

She takes and examines the card.

Well, if anyone's going to carry off a scheme like that, it certainly won't be Charlie bloody Thrupp.

Tug *laughs.* **Finty** *looks at him.*

Finty   But you know, I think it's a brilliant idea.

Tug   What, impersonating a Russian oligarch?

Finty   No, that's obviously a terrible idea. (*Handing back the card.*) I meant selling the castle.

Tug   What?

Finty   I mean, think about it, Tuggy. I get so sad, those long summer months that you're up there on your own. I know you adore that castle of yours, but that's what it is: yours. If you and I are truly going to make a life together, then we need somewhere that's both of ours. So let your mother sell the place, then let's buy a home for the two of us. Somewhere you and I can be together forever.

Tug   Forever?

Finty   Forever.

Tug   Forever?

Finty   Forever.

Tug   Forever, though?

Finty (*going in close, suddenly sharp*)   Now you listen to me, Theodore Bungay. I see that shifting glimmer of doubt in your eye. I've been engaged to you for seven long years, don't think I don't know a viscount about to weasel out of something when I see one. Sell the castle, move in with me in London, or we're done. No more sheen of affianced respectability, no more safety net of my daddy's cash. Nothing. Do you hear me?

Tug   Yes.

Finty (*suddenly bright again*)   Splendid! Oh, Tuggy-wuggy, just imagine! The cab rolling up to our cute little mews-house to take us every night to parties and balls and receptions; you presenting me, your sparkling wife, to everyone who matters, MPs, and diplomats, and theatre directors, and me never leaving your side but charming them all, as the caterers glance knowingly at each other and say 'There goes Lady Bungay. She'll run the whole show someday.' And I will. You can imagine that, can't you, Tuggy-wuggy?

Tug   I certainly can.

Finty (*sharp again*)   So make it fucking happen. (*Kissing him, back to bright.*) Listen, I have to go and prep my evening edition, but I'll see you later, okay? I love you, Tug Bungay.

Tug   I love you too, Finty Crossbell.

Finty   Forever.

Tug   Forever.

Finty   Forever.

She goes.

Tug   Forever. Forever. (*Suddenly aghast.*) Forever?! Oh God, what have I done?!

Mrs Hanratty *arrives.*

Mrs Hanratty   Everything all right, Theodore?

Tug   No, Mrs Hanratty. Everything is not all right at all.

Mrs Hanratty   Well, worry not. Just think of Tsar Nicholas the Second when he got turfed out of the Winter Palace.

Tug   Why? What happened to him?

Mrs Hanratty   Executed by firing squad.

Tug   I'm not sure that's a helpful example.

Mrs Hanratty   Can I get you a drink, then?

Tug   Thanks. How about a rather large whisky?

Mrs Hanratty   Very good, sir.

She goes. **Tug** *stands, looking distraught. Then, a sudden impulse seizes him. He pulls out the Stylist's business card and turns it over pensively in his hands, examining it.* **Mrs Hanratty** *returns with* **Tug***'s drink.*

Tug (*slowly, an idea dawning*)   On second thoughts, Mrs Hanratty, you'd better make it a vodka.

Act Two

The rose garden at Dimley Grange castle, Northumberland, the following afternoon. At stage left, a flight of stone steps leading up into the castle itself. The exit at stage right leads to a clifftop, with a view of the sea, and a steep pathway down to the beach beyond. On stage there are beautiful bushes of blooming roses and a little garden table off to the side. The weather is sunny and warm. **Agrippina Bungay** *and her native-French-speaking account manager,* **Simone Montesquieu**, *are playing badminton. They reach an appropriate point in their game and cease.*

Agrippina   I fear neither of us is, in actual fact, particularly good at badminton, Simone.

Simone   It's true. And yet we are at it almost constantly, Agrippina. I feel, therefore, that there must be some other purpose to our frequent encounters.

Agrippina   Indeed. If only we knew what it was.

Simone   If only we knew.

They look at each other intently for a moment. Then **Agrippina** *breaks off and looks at the sky.*

Agrippina   Such a delightful day, don't you think? Sunny but not too bright. Warm but not too hot. Not a breeze in the air, not a cloud in the big northern sky. Fantastic castle-selling weather.

Simone   Oh, don't speak to me of the weather, Agrippina. I detest a subtext in any conversation. Even a hint of a thought left unspoken brings out a dreadful rash on my neck.

Agrippina   Well, tell me what you're thinking, then.

Simone   I daren't, lest it disturb your delicate English aristocratic sensibility.

Agrippina   Oh, I think that could handle just a little disturbing, don't you?

Simone   It certainly could last night.

Agrippina   Oh, Simone.

Simone   Oh, Agrippina. Come to South Korea with me.

Agrippina   You know that I want to. Tell me again what it's like there.

Simone   The flats all have underfloor heating, the people display a marked deference towards their senior citizens, and the public transportation system operates twenty-four hours a day.

Agrippina   Stop it, Simone. You know there's nothing more erotic to me than well-maintained local infrastructure.

Simone   Then I shall speak to you ceaselessly of the elegance of the Seoul metropolitan bus service.

Agrippina   And I shall be reduced to a quivering puddle on the ground. But, before my imminent dissolution, there is the small matter of this place to resolve.

Simone   Oh, I wouldn't worry about that. I have the paperwork all here, prepared. And Mr Govorov will be here momentarily. So we'll get it all signed, then it should only take a second to transfer over the money from his Gibraltar-based holding account to yours, we hand over the keys, and by the end of today it's goodbye to England for you and for me, and *annyeonghaseyo* to the bullet-train to Busan.

Agrippina   I do still worry a little about Theodore, though. I haven't even told him I'm leaving the country. It may come as a significant blow for a young man to lose both his home and his mother in a single day. He may not seem so, but he's quite an uncertain soul, deep down. I don't want to leave him here on his own.

Simone   I'm sure he'll be fine. I'd give him a month or so to mope about, then it'll be back to immersive historical-themed dining experiences and virtual-reality fishing competitions or whatever it is rich young men do in London these days.

Agrippina   I hope you're right. Still, he almost despises me already. And it causes me no small amount of heartache, you know, to have an only child who thinks of me as some sort of monstrous flying gorgon. Do gorgons fly?

Simone   I believe they are winged but flightless, like the penguin.

Agrippina   Well, gorgon or penguin, I wish to be neither.

Simone   To me, you are no penguin. To me, you are like a ripe, wet fruit. And I want to peel you.

Agrippina   Oh, Simone.

Simone   Oh, Agrippina. My delicious fig.

Agrippina   My dripping nectarine.

Simone   My sopping papaya.

Agrippina   My . . . damp . . . apple, oh, kiss me, Simone!

They kiss passionately. **Mrs Hanratty** *enters carrying a big cool-box and humming the Soviet national anthem. She stops abruptly, seeing* **Simone** *and* **Agrippina** *kissing, and stands awkwardly for a moment. She coughs.*

Mrs Hanratty   Ahem!

Agrippina *and* **Simone** *notice* **Mrs Hanratty** *and break apart.*

Mrs Hanratty   I've brought a big cool-box.

Agrippina   Oh, thank you, Mrs Hanratty. Mrs Hanratty, this is Simone Montesquieu, my account fiancée. I mean, my account manager.

Mrs Hanratty   I'm pleased to see you paying so much attention to your clients, Ms Montesquieu.

Simone   Yes, my firm aims to provide a very personal service.

Mrs Hanratty   Well, I can barely get a Tuesday afternoon appointment with my own bank manager, let alone a loving embrace. Perhaps I ought to switch branches.

Simone   That could be an idea. I'll give you my contact information and we can schedule a meeting with a colleague. How much do you have in savings?

Mrs Hanratty   Oh, five, or six –

Simone   Well, I imagine we'd set you up as a limited partnership and go from there. The big money, of course, remains in central London property but there are similarly lucrative smaller avenues we can go down: student housing, say, or migrant accommodations leased back to the state. Five or six million pounds isn't a lot these days but it's not a bad beginning.

Mrs Hanratty   Oh no, you mistake me, Ms Montesquieu. I have five or six pounds in savings. Which I doubt would even be enough to purchase a low-grade breeze block for one of those refugee prisons of yours. I do beg your pardon, I mean 'migrant accommodations'.

Simone   Who is this woman, Agrippina? I thought she was your friend.

Agrippina   Oh, no, Simone, Mrs Hanratty isn't a friend. She's Theodore's superfluous housekeeper. She's providing light refreshment for the proceedings today.

Mrs Hanratty (*showing off the cool-box*)   That I am.

Agrippina   And just where is my delinquent son this afternoon?

Mrs Hanratty   He's been rather held up, I'm afraid, but he'll be along shortly. He's currently experiencing a 'wardrobe malfunction'.

Agrippina   I'm not sure I want to know about that, Mrs Hanratty.

Mrs Hanratty   Oh, I mean it quite literally in this case. He's managed to lock himself inside his walk-in wardrobe. Couldn't get out for an hour. He was supposed to meet me at King's Cross, but he's following on a few trains behind.

Agrippina   Typical Theodore. That child and door handles! Well, if Govorov arrives in the meantime, we'll just have to get started without him.

Mrs Hanratty   So where should I set up this buffet, then?

Agrippina   Well, it's such a beautiful day that I thought we'd do it just over there (*Points offstage right.*) on the clifftop, to get a nice view of the sea. You'll notice I've put up a trestle table already.

Mrs Hanratty   Sounds lovely. (*Opening the cool-box.*) I've got miniature bruschettas, and hog-roast sausage rolls, and prawn vol-au-vents, and tiny little quiches, so that should be enough for us all to be getting along with. We can even have a bit of a preview now, if you fancy?

Simone   I never say no to a tiny little quiche.

Mrs Hanratty   Oh, would you like one?

Simone   No, I am full.

Mrs Hanratty   All right, then. And finally, for the *pièce de resistance . . .*

She produces a magnificent and very fragile-looking cake replica of the castle.

Mrs Hanratty   *Le Gâteau-Château du Dimlie*! A shit-ton of cake, in the shape of your castle.

Agrippina   That's extraordinary, Mrs Hanratty.

Mrs Hanratty   Just a little something I whipped up overnight. I'll put it on the table over there, for now, then we can all have a celebratory slice once the deal's done.

She slowly and carefully carries the teetering cake over to the garden table and sets it down, placing her cake slice next to it.

There.

Agrippina   Thank you, Mrs Hanratty. Frankly, I'm amazed. I don't know if anyone's ever said this to you before, but you really ought to try out for the Bake Off.

Mrs Hanratty   No, if you'll pardon the expression, Lady Bungay: fuck that noise. Just my opinion, but that foul excuse for a television show proliferates a cloying and retrograde view of this country, which has never existed outside the brandy-addled imaginings of a red-faced racist rear admiral, and as such is tantamount to imperialist propaganda.

Agrippina   It was just a suggestion.

Mrs Hanratty   I bake for the love of it, Lady Bungay. Nothing more, nothing less.

Agrippina   I see: *crustum gratia crustis*.

Mrs Hanratty   Precisely.

Awkward silence.

I'll just go and set up the buffet.

Agrippina   Yes, good idea.

Mrs Hanratty *picks up the cool-box and exits to the clifftop side.*

Agrippina (*secretively*)   Mrs Hanratty is a communist, I'm afraid.

Simone   That makes sense. I noticed a strange propensity for sharing.

Agrippina   A worrying number of pastry chefs are, these days. These people may make a magnificent shortcrust, but you can't talk to them about anything.

Simone   A revolutionary cake-maker! Only in England!

Agrippina (*suddenly a bit anxious*)   Oh, I do hope that Theodore gets here all right on his own. He always gets confused when he has to change trains.

Simone   There's no need to be anxious, Agrippina. I'm sure that he will make it just fine.

Tug *descends the steps from the castle, disguised as a Russian oligarch. Due to the Cultural Stylist's consummate theatrical magic, the audience is aware that it's him but the other characters onstage are not. His accent and costume are pronounced but not completely ridiculous. Overall, he does a pretty good job.*

Tug   Good afternoon to you two women! My name is Oleg Mikhailovich Govorov, Russian oligarch.

Agrippina   Mr Govorov! A great pleasure to meet you, at long last. I'm Agrippina Bungay.

Tug (*bowing*)   Lady Bungay.

Agrippina   Please, call me Agrippina.

Tug   With pleasure, Agrippina. It's such a joy to meet a real-life English aristocrat! Makes me sad we Russians mercilessly liquidated all of ours.

Agrippina   It's an equal joy to meet a real-life oligarch, Mr Govorov. I've never met one before.

Tug   To be completely honest with you, neither have I!

Tug *laughs uproarious at his own joke.* **Agrippina** *and* **Simone** *laugh along nervously.*

Agrippina (*stops laughing*)   Erm, right. Well, this is Ms Montesquieu, she'll be handling the paperwork today.

Simone   Simone. If there's anything you need, Mr Govorov, please don't hesitate to ask.

Tug (*smiling*)   Oh, I don't think there'll be very much at all.

Agrippina   I trust you got here all right?

Tug   Yes, though I found the interchanges on the train to be somewhat confusing.

Simone   You took the train? I would have thought that someone of your stature would at least have a chauffeur to drive you over.

Tug   My chauffeur is currently on paternity leave. I make extremely good provision for the new parents in my employ. But I do not mind taking the train. It allows me to look out of the window while I drink four cans of lager beer, like the locals do.

Simone   Well, I'm pleased to hear that you had a pleasant journey.

Tug (*to* **Agrippina**)   You have a son, correct? Will he not be joining us?

Agrippina   I do, yes. Theodore. The viscount. He'll be along shortly.

Tug   I have heard he is very intelligent and extremely good-looking.

Agrippina   That might've been said by someone somewhere at some point.

Tug   He must be being disappointed, no, to be losing his beautiful home? Tell me, is it true that the then-future Charles the Second once stayed here when he was on the run from the Roundheads?

Agrippina   It is.

Tug   How immensely historically significant! Thirty generations in this one same family! A scrap of England's soul. Aren't you sad to see it dying away? Yes, it must be heart-breaking for your son to say goodbye to this wonderful place. Quite frankly, as his mother, I'm not sure how you could be so cruel as to do this to him.

Agrippina   Erm –

Tug   A joke, a joke. A little Russian humour. Laughter through tears. All I mean is, if this were my home, I would never be letting it go.

Agrippina   Well, it will be your home, soon enough.

Tug (*almost dropping the accent*)   We'll see about that.

Tug *glares at* **Agrippina**.

Agrippina (*confused, but keeping it together*)   Right, well, let's begin the tour, then, shall we? Welcome to Dimley Grange! This is the rose garden, which was built –

Tug   My apologies for the interruption, Lady Bungay, but I ask that you end this foul tour of yours at once. I care not a bright silver rouble for this fabulous rose garden, nor for any of the other copious charms of this magnificent property, for I wish to state clearly and definitively that I, Oleg Mikhailovich Govorov, Russian oligarch, do not want to buy this castle! Though it may represent a beauty, a joy, even a kind of peace for its putative owner, that owner, alas, will not be I. I only ask that you take my word here in person today as final, that you never again attempt to contact me or any of my representatives, and, just to foreclose all possible avenues of logic, that you treat any future calls from them as strange yet hilarious Russian jokes, and ignore them entirely. I believe I have made myself perfectly clear in my wishes, so all that remains is for me to depart. Goodbye, or, as they say in my home country of Russia, *do svidaniya!*

Tug *exits into the castle triumphantly.* **Agrippina** *and* **Simone** *look a bit stunned.*

Agrippina (*slow, despondent*)   Right. Well, I suppose that's that, then. I guess we ought to contact the folks in Busan, tell them I'm not going to make it.

Simone   No, no, Agrippina, I won't let this ruin our plans. We can still go tonight. We leave, I put the castle on the open market, and between all the additional oligarchs and Chinese businessmen and Saudi princes and infantile professional footballers about the place, I'm sure we can find another buyer quick as a flash.

Mrs Hanratty *returns from the clifftop.*

Mrs Hanratty   Right, we're all set up with the buffet over there. How's the cake looking? I'll just nip up to the kitchen and fetch a tad more icing sugar for the turrets.

Agrippina   The cake will not be necessary, Mrs Hanratty.

Mrs Hanratty   Cake is always necessary, Lady Bungay.

Agrippina   Not in this case, I'm afraid. It seems our business today has rather run aground.

Mrs Hanratty   So Mr Govorov's been here already?

Agrippina   Been and, indeed, gone.

Mrs Hanratty   Wow, that was quick. I mean, he didn't fancy any of the quiches or anything?

Agrippina   Mr Govorov fancied neither the quiches nor the rose garden, nor the castle as a whole, it would appear. He made his disinclination perfectly clear and then left.

Simone   Oh, good riddance to him, in my opinion. That philistine did not deserve the exquisiteness of Mrs Hanratty's quiche.

Mrs Hanratty   Well, I'm sorry to hear that it didn't work out for you, Lady Bungay. But if you don't mind my saying so, that's still no reason to pass up a nice piece of cake. To deny yourself a joy at a time like this strikes me as a little bit churlish. So, if it can't be celebratory cake, let it at least be commiseratory cake.

Agrippina   No, I'm sorry, Mrs Hanratty. Now the deal's off, I can hardly bear to look at it anymore. Remove the cake.

Mrs Hanratty (*sadly*)   Right you are, Lady Bungay.

Mrs Hanratty *sadly picks up the teetering cake and carefully heads into the castle.*

Simone   The radical Marxist is right. There's no need, now, for downheartedness. We still have this day, this sunshine, each other.

Agrippina   I know. But . . . there's just something about the whole thing. It just doesn't feel quite right, somehow.

Simone   How do you mean?

Agrippina   I don't know how to explain it. Something about that man. I can't quite put my finger on it.

Simone   He just seemed like a typical middle-aged Russian dissident to me.

Agrippina   He was somehow familiar.

Simone   Maybe you sat next to him in the House of Lords?

Agrippina   No, that's not it. It's probably nothing. It's probably just me. I just need to get over it, now. Govorov isn't going to buy the castle. I just need to accept it and move on.

Finty *enters, casually, from the clifftop, disguised as a Russian oligarch. Hers is a suaver and far more sophisticated* **Oleg**, *with a far less discernible accent. She holds herself calmly and confidently, gesticulating expansively with a prawn vol-au-vent as she talks.*

Finty   I hope you don't mind my intruding this way, but it was such a delicious day that I thought I'd take a brief stroll along the beach first. The sand was sparkling, the sea water was clear, this magnificent edifice cleft the sky in two, and just as I mounted the clifftop path, I saw a beautiful table laid out with all manner of exquisite baked goods and I couldn't resist helping myself.

She takes a bite out of her vol-au-vent.

Mm! These prawn vol-au-vents! Whoever concocted them ought to apply for the English Nationalistic Baking Contest. Forgive me, I haven't even introduced myself. My name is Oleg Mikhailovich Govorov, Russian oligarch.

Agrippina   Oleg Mikhailovich Govorov?

Finty   Yes, Oleg Mikhailovich Govorov, Russian oligarch.

Agrippina   But we've already met an Oleg Mikhailovich Govorov today.

Finty   Oh, have you? Well, that would be my . . . elder brother, Oleg Mikhailovich Govorov.

Simone   Your brother?

Finty   Yes.

Agrippina   And both called Oleg?

Finty   Yes. We had exceptionally unimaginative parents.

Simone   And both oligarchs?

Finty   Yes. We also had exceptionally unimaginative careers advisors.

Agrippina   But which one of you is the real Oleg Mikhailovich Govorov?

Finty   That is a question of advanced metaphysics which I, unfortunately, am unqualified to answer.

Simone   No, she means which one of you is the Russian dissident who was interested in buying this castle?

Finty   Oh. That would be my elder brother.

Agrippina   Well, I'm sad to say it, Mr Govorov, but you just missed your brother. He came, declined to go through with the purchase, and rather rapidly departed.

Finty   Oh, that sounds just like Oleg. I was suspicious he may do as much, hence why I followed him here today. He is always making wrongheaded and damaging decisions, that man. I'm sure that he actually desires the sale, if he knows what's really good for him.

Agrippina   He did seem quite certain, at the time, that he didn't want to buy it.

Finty   I wouldn't pay too much attention to that. It may shock you to learn, but my elder brother has significant intellectual, and, if I may be so candid, sexual deficiencies. I am often forced to keep his idiotic impulses in check.

Agrippina   So you think he may be convinced to reconsider the purchase?

Finty   I do. Indeed, I believe I can even bring him back to say so. I'll bet that he hasn't gone far.

Agrippina   Fantastic! Well, I don't know if there's any I can get for you in the meantime? I'm Agrippina Bungay, by the way, and this is my account manager Ms Montesquieu.

Simone   Charmed.

Agrippina   How about a little tour of the grounds? This is the rose garden, which was built –

Finty   I wouldn't say no to a few more of those heavenly vol-au-vents. The fresh seafood in this part of the country is simply phenomenal.

Agrippina   Right this way.

Finty   Wonderful.

They start to go out.

Agrippina   You have a stunning command of English, if I may say, Mr Govorov. You barely have an accent at all.

Finty   I was educated here so I speak your language perfectly. I don't know why all English people seem to think Russians must have ridiculous accents. To be perfectly frank, I find it a gauche and offensive cliché.

Finty, **Agrippina** and **Simone** *go out to the clifftop. Almost immediately,* **Tug**, *now out of his disguise and looking extremely pleased with himself, and* **Mrs Hanratty**, *descend the stairs from the castle.*

Tug Well, I thought all of that went off rather brilliantly, Mrs Hanratty. I kept gracefully in character, they bought the whole disguise, and I bloody nailed the accent, too, to be honest. And that little walk-in wardrobe bit of yours was a stroke of genius! Not too ridiculous, but exactly the kind of thing that I'd do.

Mrs Hanratty Thank you, Theodore. Though I'm not sure you should sound quite so proud of yourself for that.

Tug Well, you know what? I am proud of myself. I am! Everything's brilliant! The roses smell perfect, the afternoon sun is high in the air, and through my own marvellous wit and ingenuity, I just managed to save my family home. If that isn't cause for celebration, I don't know what is. I wonder if mother's got any champagne lying around here somewhere?

Simone *returns from the clifftop carrying an empty plate.*

Simone Ah, Mrs Hanratty, there you are, I've been sent to find you. (*Noticing* **Tug**.) And you must be Agrippina's son, Theodore. How lovely to meet you, at last. I'm Simone Montesquieu, your mother's account manager.

Tug Please, call me Tug.

Simone No, thank you.

Tug A pleasure.

Tug *extends his hands to* **Simone**.

Simone My apologies, I don't shake hands with men. Not since the pandemic.

Tug Righty-o. So you're the famous account manager, are you? Busy wiring funds and firing off mortgages left, right and centre?

Simone That isn't how mortgages work.

Tug Sorry, I have no idea about mortgages. But I hear you're giving my mother some good stroke practice?

Simone   Excuse me?

Tug   Badminton.

Simone   Ah, yes. Your mother has a beautiful wrist-flick.

Tug   That's . . . good to hear. Anyway, Mrs Hanratty was just telling me that I've already missed Mr Govorov. Such a shame! I've always wanted to see an oligarch out in the wild. I've heard he was extremely good-looking.

Simone   Really? Not my type, to be honest. His brother is by far the better looking of the two in my opinion.

Tug   His brother? They must've missed that off his Wikipedia page. I wasn't aware that he had a brother.

Simone   Neither was I, until about five minutes ago.

Tug   Those Wikipedia chaps, eh! They really are good, keeping everything so constantly updated. Most of them aren't even being paid, you know. Just doing it for the love.

Simone   No, I mean his brother arrived five minutes ago.

Tug   Arrived? Arrived where?

Simone   Arrived here. That's why I was coming to find you, Mrs Hanratty. We took Mr Govorov junior over to the buffet, where he set about completely demolishing the prawn vol-au-vents. I've never seen anything like it. We wondered if you had any more?

Mrs Hanratty   Yes, of course.

She takes the plate and exists briskly into the castle.

Tug   Prawns? Hang on a minute –

Finty *and* **Agrippina** *return, laughing with one another.*

Finty (*laughing, mid-anecdote*)   . . . So then Oleg turned, blushing, to the rest of the guests and said, 'I'm sorry, I thought that was what you were supposed to do with a swordfish!'

Agrippina (*laughing raucously*)   Oh, that's hilarious!
(*Noticing* **Tug**.) Theodore! There you are, thank goodness.
Mr Govorov was just regaling me with tales of his elder
brother's ludicrous antics.

Tug   Yes, I'm sure he kept that swordfish anecdote
completely in context.

Finty (*going over to* **Tug**)   Ah, you must be the viscount I've
heard so much about. I find you to be even punier in
person.

They shake hands.

Tug   And you must be my brother. I mean, Mr Govorov's
brother.

Finty   Oleg Mikhailovich the second! A pleasure.

They keep shaking hands for far too long.

Tug   That's strange, I presumed you'd be Russian as well.

Finty   Oh, I'm definitely Russian. (*Winking at* **Agrippina**.)
Last time I checked.

Finty *and* **Agrippina** *laugh raucously.*

Tug   No, I mean you don't have much of an accent.

Agrippina   Mr Govorov was educated in England,
Theodore. So the accent is no longer an issue.

Tug   Oh. Good. (*Looking at* **Finty**.) That's a good idea,
actually.

Agrippina   What's a good idea, Theodore?

Tug   Oh. Erm. Being educated in England. Yeah. Great
selection of unis. Where abouts was it that you went to?

Finty   Exeter.

Tug   I see. I was at Oxford, myself. The finest university in
the world, so they say.

Finty   I don't think that's true anymore. Indeed, the single stupidest person I've ever met in my life attended Oxford University. It really is no mark of calibre in a man these days. I apologise if I've offended your beloved *alma mater*.

Tug (*touching* **Agrippina** *on the shoulder*)   Don't worry, I'm sure she'll get over it. Just a little Latin joke for you there.

Finty   You speak Latin, do you? I'm glad to see your expensive education has equipped you with so many useful skills.

Tug (*grumpily*)   Well, if I'm completely honest, Mr Govorov, I think I prefer my Russians to have an accent. Shows they're making the effort somehow.

Agrippina   Theodore! There's no need to be rude to our guest.

Finty (*to* **Agrippina**)   It's fine. I've faced this kind of prejudice every day of my life. I assure you, your son's reduction of my entire country to a shallow series of postures and gestures says more about England's specific combination of superiority and narrow-mindedness than it does anything about Russia itself.

Agrippina   Well, I do hope you find us a tolerant and welcoming bunch, overall.

Finty   Oh, magnificently so! In this land a person can arrive with nothing but the shirt on his back, several billion pounds in his pocket and a rolodex of suspicious ex-KGB contacts in his bag and within just a few years his offspring can be editing national newspapers and sipping champagne with supposedly left-wing actors at their very own blood-money-funded theatre awards ceremony.

Tug   Hey, leave the thespies alone, would you? They've had a hard time of it of late. And it's nothing to do with us anyway. It's not like we're going to be winning any theatre awards any time soon.

Finty   I highly doubt we'll be nominated.

Mrs Hanratty *comes down from the castle with a fresh plateful of vol-au-vents.*

Mrs Hanratty   More vol-au-vents for our Russian guest!

Finty   Fantastic! I take it you're the chef.

Mrs Hanratty   I am. (*Handing over the vol-au-vents.*) And you must be Mr Govorov. This is so exciting! I've always wanted to meet an actual Russian. I greatly admire your culture and political history. Not so much for the last thirty years, but the stuff before that, you know. The nice Soviet stuff. Abolition of private property, five-year plans, ruthlessly purging the counterrevolutionaries, all that business.

Agrippina   Mrs Hanratty –

Mrs Hanratty   Allow me to ask you a personal question. Did you ever happen to come across a fellow by the name of Vladimir Ilych Lenin?

Agrippina   I'm not sure this is the time –

Finty   What a ridiculously xenophobic question. You think, just because I am Russian, I am supposed to know Lenin. Do you know the King of England?

Mrs Hanratty   No, but –

Tug   I actually do know the King. Haven't seen him for a bit, but –

Finty   No, I don't know Lenin! He is dead!

Mrs Hanratty   I think you're thinking about it too literally –

Simone   Perhaps we could return to the matter at hand? Mr Govorov, you suggested you may require Theodore's help in finding your brother and allowing us to resume the sale today?

Finty   Yes, I'm sure with a bit of gentle investigation we can unearth Mr Govorov senior again, no problem. He's bound to be skulking about nearby, already regretting his rashness.

Tug   Oh, I doubt that very much. That particular Oleg Mikhailovich is long gone and regret-less, I'm certain. But I wouldn't say no to a brief private word with this brother of his, anyway. You know. Man to man. Viscount to oligarch.

Agrippina   All right, then. (*Picking up the badminton rackets.*) Simone and I will be out by the buffet, working on our net-play.

Simone   Actually, Agrippina, I might just pop up to the castle, to make a quick call. I'll be with you momentarily.

Agrippina   Of course, I'll see you there. We're running rather low on sausage rolls too, Mrs Hanratty, if you get a minute. (*To* **Finty** *and* **Tug**.) I do hope you find him.

Finty   Have no fear, Lady Bungay. We'll resolve this one way or another.

Agrippina *goes out to the clifftop.* **Mrs Hanratty** *and* **Simone** *go back up the steps to the castle.* **Finty** *and* **Tug** *are left alone. A charged moment of silence.* **Finty** *munches a vol-au-vent.*

Tug   Enjoying yourself over there, are you?

Finty   I am indeed. The puff pastry is tender and light as the air, and the prawn nestled gently inside it is cold, pink and deliciously shrivelled. Just the way I like it.

Tug   I'm glad to hear it, Oleg Mikhailovich Govorov. Or should I say . . . Finty.

Finty   That's correct, Tug Bungay. Or should I say . . . Oleg Mikhailovich Govorov.

Tug   I see you wasted no time at all in whipping out The Swordfish Incident. I thought you promised never to mention that again.

Finty   I did. But Oleg Mikhailovich Govorov didn't. And I see you wasted no time at all in scuppering the sale of your castle.

Tug   I didn't. But Oleg Mikhailovich Govorov did.

Finty   Well then.

Tug   Yes.

Finty   Indeed.

Tug   Here we are.

Finty   Here we are.

Tug   A dissident double act.

Finty   A little pair of Olegs.

Into a rapid exchange:

Tug   So you paid a visit to Charlie's Cultural Stylist, did you?

Finty   So *you* paid a visit to Charlie's Cultural Stylist, did you?

Tug   Well, I didn't see that I had any other choice.

Finty   Well, *I* didn't see that *I* had any other choice.

Tug   I thought you said that impersonating an oligarch was a terrible idea.

Finty   I did. Which is exactly how I knew you were going to do it. I did what had to do to save our relationship.

Tug   I did what I had to do to save my home.

Finty   I understand that your home's important to you.

Tug   I understand that our relationship's important to you.

Finty   So you're saying our relationship isn't important to you? Fuck you, Tug!

Tug   Fuck you, Finty!

Simone *returns from the castle and observes* **Tug** *and* **Finty** *suspiciously as she crosses the stage out to the clifftop.* **Tug** *and* **Finty** *snap out of their argument.*

Tug (*for* **Simone**'s *benefit*) So the thing about Oxford, Oleg, is that people think it's one university, when it's actually comprised of forty-three separate colleges, each a kind of little university unto itself. So I was at Christ Church, which is known as 'The House' –

Finty (*as* **Oleg** *again*) And is it an actual house?

Tug More like a mini cathedral.

Finty How fascinating! I love it when English men explain facts to me.

Simone *has gone.*

Finty (*whispered*) Fuck you, Tug.

Tug (*whispered*) Fuck you, Finty.

Finty You have no idea how much I've invested in us over the years.

Tug You have no idea how much I've invested in my castle over the years!

Finty Trust me, I do. But, for crying out loud, Tuggy, you have to let it go sooner or later. It's just a place! Yes, I get it now, a truly magnificent place –

Tug Do you see what I mean about the arrow-slits?

Finty Catching the afternoon sunlight like cherubim's eyes? Yes, I do! But it's still just a place!

Tug It's not just a place! It's lots of other things too! Beautiful things! Things I don't want to explain too much right now because I don't want to sound too corny and obvious! Metaphorical things!

Finty Yeah? Well maybe I could be a metaphor too.

Tug   I'm sure that you could be, if someone out there thought hard enough about it!

Finty   Maybe you could even be one as well!

Tug   Maybe! I sure as hell hope so!

Finty   So where do we go from here, then?

Tug   I don't know. Where do you think we go from here, then?

Finty   I don't know. Where do you think I think we go from here, then?

Tug   I don't know. Where do you think I think –

Finty (*cutting through it, serious*)   It's the last time I'll say this, Tuggy. It's this place or me. That's all. So either you do the sensible thing and go and fetch your oligarch outfit and pretend to be my elder brother again, or I get them to call me a taxi to the station and I leave your life forever.

Silence.

Tug   How long have I got to think about it?

Finty *turns and starts to go.*

Tug   Wait!

Tug *runs and grabs her by the hand. She stops and looks at him.*

You like fish too much.

Silence.

Finty   You like fishing too much.

Tug   You like whining too much.

Finty   You like wine too much.

Tug   You like shots too much.

Finty   You like shooting too much.

Tug   You're classless!

Finty   You're tasteless!

Tug   Outsider!

Finty   Inbred!

Tug   Nouveau riche!

Finty   Dusty relic!

Tug   You're pretentious and ruthless and clingy and strange.

Finty   You're lazy and silly and selfish and vain.

Tug (*smiling*)   But.

Finty (*smiling*)   But.

Tug   Well.

Finty   Well.

Tug   You know.

Finty   You know.

They fall into each other's arms and kiss passionately. **Mrs Hanratty** *returns from inside the castle carrying a fresh plate of sausage rolls and humming the Soviet national anthem. She stops abruptly, seeing the kissing couple.*

Mrs Hanratty   Christ, not again. (*Coughs.*) Ahem!

Finty *and* **Tug** *notice* **Mrs Hanratty** *and break apart.*

Mrs Hanratty (*seeing it's* **Finty** *that* **Tug** *has been kissing, but still thinking it's* **Oleg**)   Oh, Mr Govorov! I didn't realise it was you.

Tug   Erm, yes, Mrs Hanratty, we were just –

Mrs Hanratty   There's no need to explain yourself, Theodore. I'm very happy for you. Indeed, I'm glad to see you've finally found someone worthy of your affections. Truth be told, I never cared much for that Finty Crossbell of yours. Sour-looking girl. Thought rather a lot of herself, with those long flowery letters she used to write. Strangely dead behind the eyes. It was almost as if you took a normal person's eyes –

Tug   Mrs Hanratty –

Mrs Hanratty   No, no, don't interrupt me, Theodore, this needs to be said. It was almost as if you took a normal person's eyes and used some sort of existential vacuum cleaner to suck all the love and humour and hope out of them, suck-suck-suck, suck-suck-suck, just like that, leaving just these hollow little lifeless globules, like you'd find on a zombie. So I'm thrilled that we don't have to deal with that any longer. And, what's more Theodore, I'm glad to see that the person you've chosen instead is, well, there's no other way of putting this, a man, because I've known you a long time, I used to change your bed for you at Oxford for crying out loud, so I think I've always been sure of where your heart truly lay. I'm made up for you is all that I'm saying. Good riddance to Finty and hello to Oleg.

Tug (*after a brief silence*)   Mrs Hanratty, this *is* Finty.

Mrs Hanratty   You what now?

Tug   This *is* Finty, Mrs Hanratty. She's in disguise, like I was.

Mrs Hanratty   Oh. Right.

Finty   Hello, Mrs Hanratty.

Mrs Hanratty (*embarrassed*)   Hello, dear. Nice to see you. How you doing?

Finty   Undead, apparently. And I believe I'll be taking a stern look at your terms of employment once Tuggy and I are married. (*Turning to* **Tug**.) Oh, please say it'll be soon, now, darling!

Tug   Of course. I'll get straight back on to searching for that photographer. Who knows, one might even have become suddenly available now!

Finty   There's also the issue of your mother's approval. I may have disguised my Englishness from her but I can't disguise the fact that I don't have a title.

Tug   Oh, I wouldn't worry too much about that. The degree to which you were able to charm her as a middle-aged Russian man bodes infinitely well for your younger, sweeter self.

Finty   Excellent, then. (*Leading* **Tug** *away towards the steps.*) Now, let us depart! I believe you're due a costume change. And I might fetch us some champagne while we're at it. Any idea where they keep it, Mrs Hanratty?

Mrs Hanratty   The filing cabinet in the office, under the tax returns. It's the one place Theodore would never think to look.

Finty   Splendid.

Mrs Hanratty   So you're off, then, are you?

Tug   Yes, Mrs Hanratty. Oleg Mikhailovich senior has had a change of heart. It seems he'll be buying the castle today after all.

Tug *and* **Finty** *go inside.* **Mrs Hanratty** *moves to take the sausage rolls out to the clifftop but is met by* **Simone** *and* **Agrippina**, *returning.*

Agrippina   There you are, Mrs Hanratty. Any news from the search party?

Mrs Hanratty   Yes, they've managed to find Mr Govorov senior, apparently. And, what's more, he's had a sudden and, in my opinion, extremely surprising change of heart.

Simone   So he's going to buy it?

Mrs Hanratty   He is.

Agrippina   Oh, fantastic! What fantastic news! This calls for a celebration, I think!

Mrs Hanratty (*eagerly*)   Shall I retrieve the cake, Lady Bungay?

Agrippina (*triumphantly*)   Retrieve the cake, Mrs Hanratty!

Mrs Hanratty   Very good, Lady Bungay.

She goes back into the castle. **Agrippina** *embraces* **Simone**.

Agrippina   Oh, relief! Relief! You know, I always knew Mr Govorov junior would come through for us like this. I always had a good feeling about that man. So confident, so calming, so witty and controlled. He reminds me a bit of myself, in my younger days.

Simone   In your younger days?

Agrippina   I don't know how to describe it. Just something about his demeanour.

Simone   Well, you have always been confident, calming, witty and controlled to me, Agrippina, and you will be until you are a foul and putrid corpse.

Agrippina   Oh, Simone! Look at me, darling.

They look at each other.

I'm free!

They hold hands happily.

Tonight. Let's go tonight.

Simone   I'm glad it all worked out in the end. Thank goodness for the Brothers Govorov, eh?

Agrippina   The Brothers Govorov. I think I read that one at university. Lots of stuff about Jesus.

Simone   Yes, except in that case, there were three of them.

Agrippina   How do you mean?

Simone   I mean, the Brothers Karamazov. There were three.

Charlie Thrupp *steams down the steps from the castle, disguised as a Russian oligarch. His* **Oleg** *is, inevitably, an absurd and completely over-the-top caricature.*

Charlie   By the Bronze Horseman of Saint Petersburg, I will not do it! By the Peter and Paul Fortress, by the Moika Embankment, by the Admiralty spire, which was built between 1806 and 1823, by the bright banks of the fast-flowing River Neva, which freezes over in the winter to allow for ice skating, by the green Winter Palace, by the main commercial thoroughfare Nevsky Prospekt, named for the thirteenth-century hero Aleksandr Nevsky, by Ivan the Terrible's crown, by Catherine the Great's crinoline, by Pushkin's sideburns, Rasputin's loincloth, Trotsky's glasses, Stalin's moustache, Gorbachev's birthmark, and the current fascist president's laughably diminutive stature, I will not buy this castle today!

During **Charlie**'s *tirade,* **Tug**, *now back in his oligarch outfit, and* **Mrs Hanratty**, *carrying the cake, which somehow looks even more magnificent and fragile than before, return from the castle.*

Agrippina   I beg your pardon, sir. Who on earth are you?

Charlie   Why, Oleg Mikhailovich Govorov, of course! Russian oligarch.

Tug (*intervening as* **Oleg**)   My apologies, Lady Bungay. This is my other brother, Oleg.

Charlie (*turning to see* **Tug**)   My brother is here?! I see my plan to attend today wasn't so 'ridiculous' after all!

Simone   Your brother?

Tug *and* **Charlie**   Yes.

Agrippina   And also called Oleg?

Tug *and* **Charlie**   Yes. (*In remarkably perfect unison.*) We had exceptionally unimaginative parents.

They look at each other, shocked but impressed by their unison.

Mrs Hanratty (*putting the cake back on the garden table*) Oh, thank goodness, a genuine Russian at last. Do *you* happen to know a fellow by the name of Vladimir Ilych Lenin?

Charlie Actually, I do!

Agrippina (*agitated*) I'm sorry, I'm finding this all more than slightly confusing. Exactly which one of you gentlemen is it that's buying the castle?

Tug That would be me. I apologise for my brother here, he just gets very invested in things.

Agrippina (*to* **Tug**) And we were told you've changed your mind, and have decided to go through with the sale, is that true?

Tug It is.

Agrippina Well, thank heavens for that.

Charlie Hang on a minute, he's decided to go through with the sale? My Oleg Mikhailovich? My big, strapping, beautiful brother Oleg Mikhailovich has decided to deprive a true-born Englishman of his history? Of his peace? No, no, I don't know about you, but that's not something the Oleg Mikhailovich I know would do, is it, Oleg Mikhailovich?

Tug *considers.*

Tug Actually, I agree with my brother.

Simone Which brother?

Tug My new one. I mean, this one. I have decided to change my mind about changing my mind. I don't know what's come over me, but I find myself suddenly very nostalgic for my home. It's a peculiarly Russian emotion but one I feel very strongly. So, no. I am sorry for all the shenanigans but I won't be buying the castle today, after all.

Agrippina Oh, for goodness' sake, this is getting ridiculous now. Remove the cake, Mrs Hanratty.

Mrs Hanratty *goes to pick up the cake.* **Finty** *rushes back in with a bottle of champagne.*

Finty   You leave that exquisite piece of baking architecture right where it is! (*To* **Charlie**.) I should've known you'd somehow slither your way into this, Oleg Mikhailovich, you arrogant snake!

Charlie   And if it isn't my brother, Oleg Mikhailovich, the duplicitous she-tiger, I mean, he-tiger, I mean, what do I mean?

Finty   I won't let you sabotage my future, Oleg Mikhailovich! The deal's still on! Replace the cake, Mrs Hanratty!

Charlie   Absolutely not, Oleg Mikhailovich! The deal is off! Remove the cake, Mrs Hanratty!

Finty   Replace the cake!

Charlie   Remove the cake!

Finty *and* **Charlie** *grab the cake tray at opposite ends and begin a frantic tug-of-war over the cake.* **Mrs Hanratty** *remains in the middle, attempting to steady it. The cake wobbles and teeters all the while.*

Finty   Replace the cake!

Charlie   Remove the cake!

Tug (*running to help* **Mrs Hanratty**)   Mind out for the cake!

Finty   The deal is on!

Charlie   The deal is off!

Finty   It's on!

Charlie   It's off!

Finty   On!

Charlie   Off!

Amid the fray, the real **Oleg Mikhailovich Govorov,** *an actual Russian, descends the stairs, sheepishly, from the castle. He is mild-mannered, softly spoken and casually dressed. Everyone sees him and freezes.*

Oleg   Erm, hello to you all. I'm looking for an Agrippina Bungay. We had a meeting today, which I chose to cancel, but, as I was sitting in my hotel room nearby just now, one of my assistants relayed a disturbing voicemail from Lady Bungay's account manager. Something about confirming my number of brothers. So I decided to sneak away from my security detail and take a taxi over here anyway, to assure her that, whatever's going on, I am still very much intending to buy. Is Lady Bungay here? My name is Oleg Govorov, by the way.

Mrs Hanratty *places the cake decisively back on the garden table.*

Agrippina   I couldn't care less who you are. As long as you have the money, I'll sell you the castle.

Oleg   My account is prepared. The funds are in place.

Agrippina (*business-like, taking him aside*)   Good. Let's get to it, then. This is the rose garden, which was built –

Tug (*desperately trying to claw it back*)   Wait! There must be some sort of mistake! I'm Oleg Mikhailovich Govorov.

Oleg   No, I'm Oleg Mikhailovich Govorov.

Charlie (*stepping forward*)   No, I'm Oleg Mikhailovich Govorov.

Finty (*stepping forward*)   No, I'm Oleg Mikhailovich Govorov.

Tug   I'm Oleg Mikhailovich Govorov!

Oleg   I'm Oleg Mikhailovich Govorov!

Charlie   I'm Oleg Mikhailovich Govorov!

Finty   I'm Oleg Mikhailovich Govorov!

Oleg *and* **Charlie** *and* **Tug** *and* **Finty** (*in perfect unison*)   I'm Oleg Mikhailovich Govorov! I'm Oleg Mikhailovich Govorov! What are you doing? Why are you speaking at the same time as me? Stop speaking at the same time as me! Stop it! Stop it! I'm Oleg Mikhailovich Govorov! I'm Oleg Mikhailovich Govorov!

A dangerous-looking **Assassin** *enters from the clifftop.*

Assassin   Good afternoon. I'm looking for an Oleg Mikhailovich Govorov.

Silence.

Oleg Mikhailovich Govorov?

Finty (*stepping back*)   Not me!

Tug (*stepping back*)   Not me!

Charlie (*stepping back*)   Not me!

Oleg (*stepping back*)   Not me!

Finty (*pointing up the line*)   It's him.

Tug (*pointing up the line*)   It's him.

Charlie (*pointing up the line*)   It's him.

Oleg (*pointing back down the line*)   It's him.

The **Assassin** *rolls their eyes and pulls out a silenced pistol.*

Assassin   Look, I don't have time for people being annoying. The president gave me a job to do. So, we can do it the difficult way or the very difficult way.

Charlie (*striking forward heroically*)   Don't worry, I'll handle this. (*Prostrates himself feebly and attempts to speak Russian.*) Erm, please, friend, pozhalsta, por favor, no hurto me, no hurto me, do svidanyia, vodka, Dostoevsky, no hurto, por favor!

Assassin   What's this idiot babbling on about?

Tug (*whispering*)   I thought you knew fluent Russian, Charlie!

Charlie (*whispering back*)   I do! (*Back to his 'Russian'.*) Vodka, blinis, Anna Karenina, caviar, Moscow, vodka, no hurto, Three Sisters, por favor!

Assassin   I speak English, you twat!

Charlie (*turning to the rest of them, like an interpreter*)   It's okay, everyone, they say they speak English!

Assassin (*cocking the pistol*)   Right. We're done here.

Oleg *steps forward calmly.*

Oleg   Erm, all right, everybody. I just wanted to say, thanks so much for the hospitality. I've had a truly fantastic day. (*Sighs.*) I've had a truly fantastic life.

He takes off his watch, his shoes and his jacket and arranges them carefully on the ground.

(*Disrobing.*) But there must be a twilight to all things. We all must face our sunset sometime. So, now, if I may.

He takes in his surroundings.

(*Overwhelmed.*) Oh, this place!

He smiles.

You are very lucky.

He begins to dance. It is slow, at first, then gradually escalating in speed and intensity. It is surprisingly graceful and beautiful. Sad but full of life. **Oleg** *dances out towards the clifftop.*

(*Leaving.*) Goodbye!

He leaps quickly out. Everyone watches him go.

Tug   No, don't go that way, that's the –

Everyone, except the **Assassin***, gasps.*

Tug   Cliff.

Silence.

Charlie (*softly, to* **Tug**)   What's down the bottom, there?

Tug   Rocks. Just. Big. Sharp. Rocks.

Assassin   Annoying. I'll have to scrape him up later. Now, let's continue.

Agrippina (*panicked*)   No, wait, he's gone now. Can't you let us go?

Assassin   Sorry, it doesn't really work like that. No loose ends, you see. My colleague – we come in pairs, you know – has already doused your whole place in gasoline and put plastic explosives in the foundations. So your home should come down pretty quickly. And then we'll burn your corpses when we're done. A tragic English castle fire. Such a shame.

A **Second Assassin** *emerges from the shrubbery.*

Assassin   Oh, there you are, Natasha. (*Pointing at* **Charlie**.) Do this one first. He's very annoying.

The **Second Assassin** *pulls out a wire and begins to garrotte* **Charlie**.

Tug   Charlie!

Mrs Hanratty *springs into action, grabs her sharpened cake slice and stabs the* **Second Assassin** *to death. It takes the first* **Assassin** *a while to realise what's going on, and by the time they do,* **Mrs Hanratty** *is moving towards them. The* **Assassin** *fires their pistol,* **Mrs Hanratty** *appears to dodge the bullet, and plunges the cake slice into the* **Assassin**'s *neck. The* **Assassin** *dies.* **Mrs Hanratty** *stands, panting. Everyone else looks extremely shocked.*

Mrs Hanratty (*panting*)   Don't worry. I'll do the tidying up.

Tug (*putting his hand on her shoulder*)   We can help, Mrs Hanratty. There's not that much to do.

The cake-castle suddenly collapses.

Mrs Hanratty   No!

The real castle explodes.

Tug   No!

Tug *tries to run inside, but* **Charlie** *holds him back. Then* **Tug,**
Charlie, **Finty**, **Agrippina**, **Simone** *and* **Mrs Hanratty** *move*
as far from the fire as they can and huddle together. They watch the
flames rise.

Agrippina   It really is just a little bit magnificent, isn't it?

They watch for a while, in various states of wonder and awe and
despair, as Dimley Grange castle burns to the ground.

Act Three

Two hours later. Just as the **Assassin** *predicted, Dimley Grange castle has disintegrated unusually quickly in the flames and is now a charred and desolate ruin. Dotted amid the wreckage, seated on fresh piles of rubble, or leaning against broken bits of masonry, are* **Tug**, **Charlie**, **Finty**, *and* **Mrs Hanratty**. *Their clothes are ripped and soot-covered, oligarch disguises tattered and at least partially compromised, some of them are huddled in blankets and they all still look quite shocked. There is a growing twilight quality to this scene.*

Charlie (*starting slowly, more lyrically, his Russian accent markedly less caricatured than before*)   It's the summers, I think. They're what I miss the most. When people imagine Russia they always see winters, they think of thick icicles, vast wastes of tundra in the low grey light, onion domes glinting in the snow, but for me it was always the summers, the hot dusty roads, the river clear in the heat and lined with ice-cream stalls, yes, it's the summers I think of when I think of my home. I was born on the twenty-second of March 1969, in the town of Dubrovka, Leningrad Province, USSR. Dubrovka is small, known mainly for its heroism in the Great Patriotic War, when it formed part of the Red Army frontline, as the German fascists pushed to circle Leningrad. As a child I would hear endlessly of the many heroes of our town, and find frequent bullet-casings, trench shovels, even the big tracks of tanks, down in the sludge by the edge of the river. A friend when I was twelve lost his leg to a leftover landmine. Another went blind by a shell. So, in that sense, I suppose, I was lucky, growing up. I was an only child. My father, Mikhail Petrovich, was an electrical engineer, and my mother, Maria Alexandrovna, was a renowned and decorated fighter pilot who, following the war, mainly made raspberry jam. Tales of my mother's extraordinary wartime exploits, which included over two hundred and twenty dogfight kills, were told widely in the locality, and even appeared depicted on one of a selection of postage stamps commissioned to commemorate the thirty-year anniversary of the end of the war, her beautiful hair poking shyly from underneath her flying helmet, her goggles on her head, her shining face upturned to the sky, proud of all she had done to repel the restless invader. And my father was proud of her, too, indeed my whole family was just so proud of her, all of them, except for me. It was 1977 and I was an eight-year-old boy whose mother was a local superhero, but whose status as such only brought into sharper relief my own relative physical weakness, high tinny voice, froglike walk and unhandsome bespectacled face. This made me a prime target for that perennial scourge of the eight-year-old boy, the nine-year-old boy. There was one particular nine-year-old, a fat rottweiler of a child named Vasya Fomkin, who used to have his malevolent entourage hold me down while he did unspeakable things to my thighs with a mathematics textbook, reciting a list of my mother's many medals as he did so. In order to avoid these regular beatings, which inevitably took place once the school day was over, I had devised a complex and extensive walk home, a long and unpredictable circumambulation of the town of Dubrovka, which, in its length and unpredictability, as well as in its evasion of all the main thoroughfares and points of interest for nine-year-old boys, would leave me certain both of escaping the daily assault of Vasya Fomkin, and of not getting home till it was very, very dark. On just this particular day, however, a beautiful hot afternoon in the first flush of summer, I could no longer bear, as my itinerary had instructed, to hide for a full twenty-five minutes behind the bins out the back of the *gastronom*, but feeling instead a yearning thirst in the back of my throat which could only be slaked by a fresh scoopful of Soviet ice-cream, I decided to risk everything, and make a break for one of the stalls which lined the banks of the vast Neva river. I picked up the pace, towards my destination. I rounded the corner quickly, onto the embankment boulevard and saw the way ahead of me was clear, not a nine-year-old in sight. I could almost taste that gooey cloudlike coldness in my mouth. I switched to a run, pre-emptively jangling the few small coins in my shorts pocket as I did, arrived at the stand and was just about to place my longed-for order when somehow, out of seemingly nowhere, Vasya Fomkin and his adjutants materialised, the entourage already reaching for my shoulders and spindly calves, the grinning, sweaty Fomkin already holding the mathematics textbook aloft and prepared in his big meaty hand, when suddenly – *thwack!* – the ice cream vendor had bounded acrobatically over his cart and swished the steel ice-cream scoop into the side of Fomkin's fat dog head, then he twirled and thrashed several times again, beating the entourage back and away. Fomkin touched his scalp and looked confused, a bright trail of blood ran down his child's face, he burst into the kind of babyish tears he'd so frequently elicited from me in the past, and fled, followed swiftly by his crew. Then the vendor walked calmly back behind his cart, wiped his bloody scoop off with a napkin, and asked what I wanted to eat. It was only then that I noticed the vendor himself for the very first time. I'd visited this cart many times in the past with my parents and it was normally staffed by a large Latvian former opera singer, known affectionately as 'Big Brunhilda', but the man who operated it today I'd never seen before. He was slim, of smallish height, bald and with a familiar-looking goatee beard surrounding his lips and chin. I thought it was unusual, too, given the hot weather, that he was wearing a thick rain mackintosh over a full business suit, and that his complexion was severely, indeed almost deathly, pallid. His bright eyes sparkled disarmingly. I ordered a strawberry ice-cream and ventured to introduce myself. 'Good afternoon, sir,' I said. 'My name is Oleg Mikhailovich Govorov.' 'Hello, little boy,' he replied, his voice piercing, yet warm. 'I'm Vladimir Ilych Lenin.' Naturally, my first question to him was what was he doing here today in our little Dubrovka, given that he was currently supposed to be 731 kilometres away in Red Square, lying in permanent state, watched constantly by elite guards and visited by a never-ending stream of well-wishers and adherents, to say nothing of the fact that he was technically, at this point, deceased. He smiled and told me he just really liked ice-cream, before intimating that the guards who were supposed to be watching him were not, in fact, as elite as was generally advertised, and it was easy enough to slip out without too much of a problem, between their shift patterns. So then I asked him what his favourite kind of ice-cream was and he said 'strawberry', and then I asked him what he thought of Dubrovka and he said 'nice', and then I asked him if he felt this Soviet Union of his had been a success overall as a political project, a prodigiously perspicacious question for an eight-year-old, I'll admit, but, then again, I was a prodigiously perspicacious eight-year-old, and he turned away in silence for a moment and set his eyes on a white swan alighting on the far bank of the river, and then he looked back at me and said, 'Like anything, of course, it has its shortcomings. But mostly it's too early to tell.' And I asked him when we would know and he said, 'There will be a war. And then there will be another. Then another and another and another. And when every lord has gone, and all is level again, then we will know. But first, there must be war.' And both of us looked at the swan. And then he left. And next time I went back to the stall, Big Brunhilda had returned, and I never saw him again. But I always remembered what he said to me, that day. I remembered it when I bought my first ice hockey team. When I first felt the wheels of my sleek private plane lift smoothly up from the runway, into the air, away from my homeland forever. And you'd better believe I remembered it when I set up a series of offshore accounts and trusts to ensure that my thoroughly undeserving children receive every penny of my riches when I die. You see I am a lord now, and you all may judge me for that. But I tell you this: I have eaten in the best restaurants in the world. I have had all manner of rich delicacies prepared for my palate by the world's finest celebrity chefs. But nothing on earth, to me, has ever tasted so sweet, as the ice-cream given to me by Vladimir Ilych Lenin, that hot summer's day, in Dubrovka.

Silence.

Tug I don't think you need to keep pretending to be an oligarch anymore, Charlie. The game's rather up on that front, I fear.

Charlie (*ditching the accent*)   Oh, I know. I was just relishing staying in character. And it felt like a shame not to make use of the backstory, you know.

Finty   Oh, I'm not so sure, I was quite enjoying you as an oligarch there, Charlie. You seemed rather dashing to me.

Charlie   Thank you, Finty. I appreciate that.

Silence.

Finty   So, how's everyone thinking of getting home, then? Taxis to the station all round?

Tug   It may have escaped your notice, Finty, but we're in rather a deep signal hole out here.

Finty   I know that, Tug. Hence your handy failure to communicate with me while you were up here every summer. I meant there must be a landline around, mustn't there?

Agrippina *and* **Simone** *arrive, looking stylish and composed, ready for the road.*

Tug   Oh, mother, there you are. I almost didn't recognise you. You're looking remarkably . . . fresh. We're trying to find a landline. There's one around here somewhere, isn't there?

Simone   There is, but I presume the assassins snipped it as a prelude to their assault on the castle.

She pulls a telephone out of the rubble and puts the receiver to her ear.

They did. How predictable.

Finty   Still, it almost beggars belief that none of the emergency services or local community appear to have noticed a significant Norman castle flaming on their horizon.

Simone   If the current statistics are to be believed, we may expect a lone ambulance to trundle up here in a week or two.

Charlie   And it's Wimbledon at the moment, isn't it? The locals are probably all watching that.

Mrs Hanratty   Or maybe they just don't care and they hate you.

Tug   Thanks for that, Mrs Hanratty. I imagine I'll stick around in the area for a while, anyway. Check into the hotel Oleg Mikhailovich was staying in and wait till the castle insurance kicks in, so I can get on with the rebuild. I'm currently thinking of going full Grand Designs on the thing. You know, leaving the ruins just where they are, but adding lots of glass, concrete floors, steel girders, multiple kitchen islands. Creating a bit of stylish modern open-plan living but with a knowing hat-tip to the original historic heritage, as it were.

Agrippina   Castle insurance? What on earth are you talking about?

Tug   What on earth are *you* talking about? Don't tell me there's no such thing as castle insurance.

Agrippina   Of course there's such a thing as castle insurance. But you don't imagine Dimley Grange had enough money left over to cover the premiums, do you? I told you, you spent it all.

Tug   Right. So that's just . . . it, then, is it? This castle's gone for good.

Agrippina   I'd have thought you'd be almost pleased, Theodore.

Tug   Pleased?!

Agrippina   Well, at least this way you're not betraying your ancestors' legacy by seeing it sold. No: burned to the ground by foreigners in an act of proprietorial violence. There's an almost poetical symmetry to that. Thaddeus Aloyisius De Bungaie would be proud.

Tug   So it's back to Chelsea for me, then, I guess? To live out my days in cramped urban ignominy.

Agrippina   Or at least till the end of the month, when the bank takes your flat.

Tug   What? They can't just confiscate the Lad Pad, who do they think they are?

Agrippina   They're the National Westminster Bank, Theodore. And that so-called 'Lad Pad' of yours is mortgaged against this castle. Which, the last time I checked, was a charred and smoking heap of masonry.

Tug   Well, can't we do something about that? Can't we call someone? Can't you get Simone over there to whip up a few more mortgages for us?

Agrippina   That isn't how mortgages work.

Tug   Why does everyone keep expecting me to know how mortgages work?! Come on, mother! I don't know how you could possibly be keeping so calm about this! We don't have any money, what are we going to do?!

Agrippina   No.

Tug   No?

Agrippina   No. *You* don't have any money. You.

Silence.

Tug   I beg your pardon?

Agrippina   As relict of the late Lord Bungay I maintain for myself a modest stipend, as stipulated by your father's will. My costs, in wild contrast to yours, are low, and so it has accumulated over the years, allowing for Simone to set up a modest investment portfolio in my name, the returns on which, of late, have been, to say the least, extremely healthy.

Simone (*winking at* **Mrs Hanratty**)   Migrant accommodations.

Tug   So why were you selling the castle, if you didn't need the money?

Agrippina   Theodore, we weren't selling it for me. Simone and I had to find some way of keeping you financially solvent.

Tug   What's that racket-wielder got to do with anything?

Agrippina   Simone and I are in love, Theodore. And we're getting married.

Tug   And just when were you planning on telling me this?! Jesus, not telling your own son you're engaged: this is a new low even for you, mother!

Agrippina   I always aimed to tell you as soon as I could, Theodore. But, as you may be aware, it's been rather an eventful day.

Tug   Well, I hasten to say that I do not approve!

Agrippina   Theodore, if you're somehow offended that I have entered into an homosexual relationship –

Tug   No, of course it's not that, mother. Goodness, no. I went to boarding school for crying out loud! It's just. Well. (*Points at* **Simone**.) Look at her. She's just a bit of a cold fish, in my opinion.

Simone   What? How dare you say that to me! I'll have you know that I am an extremely hot fish. Tell him, Agrippina.

Agrippina   Simone's right, Theodore. She's an extremely hot fish.

Tug   If you say so, mother.

Simone (*holding her hand*)   Come on, Agrippina. It's time to go. Our flight from Newcastle leaves in less than four hours and I want to get to the airport early so I can browse all of the miniature toiletries.

Tug   What?! You're leaving the country, as well?!

Agrippina   Yes. I do understand that this may be a lot to take in. But Simone and I are lucky enough to been offered the co-stewardship of a prestigious racket sports academy in Busan, South Korea.

Tug   Right, well, that's completely bananas. I didn't even think you were that good at badminton! You only started playing it about six months ago.

Simone   It's largely an administrative position.

Agrippina   But it commences immediately and we fully intend to take it up. I'd meant to finalise the sale of the castle before our departure, for the sake of your financial prospects, but it appears to have finalised itself in a different way entirely, here today. So, it's a flight from Newcastle to Amsterdam this evening, then on to South Korea bright and early tomorrow morning. (*Sighing.*) Ugh, I'm glad to be on my way. I'd love to say that I'll miss this strange little England of ours, with its difficult taps, its narrow houses, its capricious weather, its substandard fruit, its sewage-strewn beaches, its psychotic history, its erratic buses, its expensive electricity, its incontinent dogs, its mindless laws, its useless government, its spineless opposition, its arrogant landscapes, and its thoroughly tasteless bread, but that would be a lie.

Tug (*sarcastically*)   Aww, you've gone all sentimentally patriotic in your old age, mother. Brings a tear to my eye.

Agrippina   Oh, don't be so unnuanced, Theodore. Of course I'm a patriot. I couldn't possibly hate this place so much if I didn't love it at least a little bit to begin with.

Tug   Wait, how are you even getting out of here?

Agrippina   Oh, Simone has her motorbike parked near the front.

Tug (*to* **Simone**)   Your motorbike? You kept that one quiet. Can't I come in the sidecar?

Simone   The sidecar is reserved for my wine.

Tug   So what am I supposed to do?!

Agrippina   Well, maybe this will give you the kick up the backside you need to finally get a job.

Tug   But I do have a –

Agrippina   Not 'having lunch'. One with a wage.

Tug   I don't know how I'd do that. I fear I lack the transferrable skills.

Agrippina   Then take a leaf out of your mother's book and marry up. I see at least two candidates amid the present company who would suffice.

Finty   Well, Tuggy and I have been engaged for seven years, Lady Bungay. We were always waiting on your approval.

Agrippina   What's that, darling?

Tug (*evasive*)   Erm, I don't think we really need to talk about this right now, shall we talk about something else?

Finty (*to* **Agrippina**)   Because that's what you always said, wasn't it? That you wouldn't see Tuggy wed any lower than an Honourable. I'm Finty Crossbell, by the way. Your son's fiancée.

Agrippina (*to* **Tug**)   Ah, I see you're involved in a secret engagement all of your own, Theodore. Well, if you expected me to feel sorry for you I certainly don't anymore. (*To* **Finty**.) Pleased to meet you, Finty. I said nothing of the sort.

Finty   What?

Tug   I think there's been some sort of misunderstanding, everybody –

Agrippina   I said nothing of the sort, darling. Do you seriously think me capable of such antediluvian prejudices? I couldn't care less who Theodore marries. What do you take me for? Some kind of snob?

Finty   So you don't disapprove of our marriage?

Agrippina   Of course not. As far as I'm concerned, he'd be more than lucky to have you. You seem like a lovely girl, beneath the middle-aged Russian disguise.

Simone (*touching her arm*)   Agrippina, we really must be going.

Agrippina   Yes, yes.

Simone   Goodbye, then, viscount. A word or two of advice before I go. (*Looks at him.*) Actually, no, I can't be bothered. We'll send you a wedding invitation from Busan. (*Pointedly.*) I'll make sure we serve fish.

She goes. **Agrippina** *starts after her.*

Tug (*really trying hard*)   No, no, wait, mummy, don't go. You can't just leave me here on my own like this.

Agrippina   You know, I didn't want to. I could hardly even face the idea this morning. But then when I thought that the deal was finally done, I felt such a huge relief rush over me. Perhaps now I can finally be myself, whoever she is. I'm quite keen to find out.

Tug   But *I* don't want to be someone else! I did it for half an hour today and I wasn't very good at it! Please, mummy, I'm scared!

Agrippina (*sharp*)   Good. It's good that you're scared. You know, your grandfathers fashioned the whole world, just so you could be exactly as you are. It was everyone else who always had to pretend. Maybe it's your turn now. Goodbye, Theodore. (*Just a little tenderness.*) Tug.

She goes.

Tug (*after them*)   No, wait, come back here! Come back here right now! Mummy, come back! (*Seething.*) Oh, the betrayal! The subterfuge! The deceit! The deceit and the lies!

He turns and is faced with a furious **Finty**.

Tug (*sheepishly*)   Oh, hey, Finty.

Finty (*angry*)   So your mother didn't say no, then?! Oh, Jesus, what have I been doing for the last seven years?!

Tug (*hangdog*)   I'm very sorry, Finty.

Finty   And I bet you could find an available photographer after all, couldn't you?

Tug   Yes, there are, in actual fact, really quite a lot of them about.

Finty   Unbelievable!

Tug   But that was before! I choose you now!

Finty   Well, of course you choose me now your castle's a big pile of rubble!

Tug   No, I chose you before it was a big pile of rubble! In the rose garden, remember? When I changed my mind about selling the castle, for you!

Finty   Yes, and then you changed your mind about changing your mind.

Tug   And now I'm changing my mind about changing my mind about changing my mind!

Finty   And how long before you change it again? You were just playing for time, Tuggy. Come to think of it, playing for time is all you've ever done. But now your time's run out. With me, at least. It was long. (*Smiling sadly.*) And it wasn't all bad. But, there we are. It's over.

Tug   No. Categorically, no, I'm afraid. It isn't over. It'll be over when I say it's over and, as far as I'm concerned, we're very much still on!

Finty   Here he is: the Viscount Theodore Bungay: lazy and silly and selfish and vain.

Tug   I thought you liked those things about me!

Finty   Maybe, for a time, I did. Or I liked that you might change. But now I see you never, ever will. In some ways it's actually rather sweet.

Tug (*hopeful*)   So you think I'm sweet, then?

Finty   Not in that way, though.

Tug   But I *can* change, Finty. I promise you, I can. (*Trying to change.*) Look, I'm changing. (*Straining hard, his voice going weird.*) I'm changing, can't you see?

Finty   We're done, Tuggy.

Tug   No. You're not leaving me too! What about our life together? The mews-house, the parties, the balls? Me introducing you to MPs and diplomats and theatre directors?

Charlie (*stepping in, surprisingly gallant*)   You heard her, Tug. Just leave her be.

Finty   Thank you, Charlie. I appreciate that.

Finty *and* **Charlie** *look at each other, but* **Tug** *intervenes.*

Tug   Oh, Charlie, mate, yeah, I forgot you were here too! Charlie, of course! I'd actually been meaning to talk to you, you know? So. We've known each other for a very long time, I mean, you're my oldest and dearest friend, so I'm definitely not indifferent to you, and I feel like you're definitely not indifferent to me, either. In fact, well, they say that you should marry your best friend, don't they, so given that you're that to me, maybe it's possibly, you know, actually quite a practical idea? I've always trusted you, and supported you, and respected you, and you know there were all those times when we had one too many Jägermeisters, and we ended up going back to mine, and doing some, you know, stuff, and then in the morning I laughed and said I couldn't remember it, well I actually could remember it, I could remember every single time, and I've been thinking about those times a lot recently, particularly, you know, very, *very* recently, and thinking that they were really quite great, so I suppose what I'm asking you, Charlton Thrupp the Third, is . . . will you marry me? Will you marry me, Charlie? (*Realises he should be kneeling, so does so.*) Will you marry me, mate?

Charlie (*moved*)   Oh, how often I've dreamed of hearing those very words from you, Tuggy! Oh, how often I've lain awake restless, under the broad canopy of the Mongolian stars or stretched out on a fishing skiff as it bounced down the Straits of Gibraltar and wondered what it would be like to hear that magical question pop from your lips.

Tug   Oh, great, then. Well, shall I get back on with finding a photographer?

Charlie   But I've realised something, Tug. Just today, in fact. You know, I always believed that I had my adventures for your sake. That somehow if my exploits abroad were bold and brave enough, you'd finally see me for who I really was, and acknowledge your true feelings. But today, as I single-handedly fought off those murderous attackers and saved all of us from certain, painful death, it was a thrill I knew you could never give me, and I've never felt more alive. So, no, I won't marry you, Tug Bungay, because I can finally say: I don't need you. The adventure itself is enough.

Tug   But it wasn't you who saved us today, Charlie.

Charlie   Oh, tell that to the fact-checkers at my publisher, Tug.

Tug   But what about staying here, with me, in the country, and settling down to a life of politics?

Charlie   I think all this (*The ruined castle.*) is taking 'rustic charm' a little too far, don't you? And besides, all that Barbour-jacketed patrician stuff feels very 2010s. I'm thinking of reinventing myself as a compassionate centrist. I've sniffed the way the wind's blowing, Tug, and it's right down the middle. (*Changing as he talks.*) This country needs someone sensible, someone direct. Inward-listening but outward-looking. Of course, on that score, it helps that I have such extensive foreign travel experience and speak so many other languages fluently.

Tug (*getting angrier*)   Ugh, you don't speak any other languages fluently, Charlie! You just wave your arms around wildly while you spout a selection of clichés broadly associated with whatever culture it is that you're currently shamelessly appropriating!

Charlie (*hurt*)   I don't know who died and made you assistant professor of linguistics. I communicate, is my point.

Tug (*nasty*)   Oh, you're a fucking joke, Charlie. A ridiculous fucking joke.

Charlie (*hardening*)   Wow. I see.

Finty   You're wrong, Tug. He's brave. And eloquent. And cultured. And resourceful and connected. He's lived a full and magnificent life. And he's found someone else now, anyway.

She cosies up to **Charlie**.

Charlie   Has he? I mean, have I? Oh, no, mate, you've got the wrong end of the stick there, I'm afraid. I'm as gay as the bright morning sun.

Finty   I know you are, Charlie. But Oleg Mikhailovich Govorov isn't.

Charlie (*back to* **Oleg** *voice, shyly*)   Well, in that case, my friend, I'm flattered, but . . .

Finty (*back to* **Oleg** *voice, seductively*)   So shy! It's funny, Oleg. I always had you pegged for an arrogant snake. But now I'll have you . . . pegged . . . for something else entirely.

Charlie (**Oleg** *voice, eagerly*)   Let's have dinner when we get back to London.

Finty (**Oleg** *voice*)   That would be my pleasure.

Charlie (*back to* **Charlie** *voice*)   Well, it may be sooner than you think . . .

The sound of helicopter blades in the distance, getting closer.

Yes, I believe that's my ride.

Tug   Your ride? What are you talking about?

Charlie   I gave the lads at RAF Boulmer a quick ring on my satellite phone while you were off hunting for Charles the Second's nightstand. Asked them to send over a Chinook for me and a friend. We should be back in London by ten. (*Turning to* **Finty**, *in* **Oleg** *voice.*) So, dinner, Oleg Mikhailovich?

Finty (**Oleg** *voice*)   Absolutely, Oleg Mikhailovich. Though I'm not sure anywhere will let us in, looking like this.

Charlie (**Oleg** *voice*)   Oh, I think I know just the place. Nice little spot down in Mayfair. Though you'd best brush up on your oil fields first.

A Chinook helicopter hovers, low and loud, overhead. The pilot drops two abseil ropes into the ruins. **Charlie** *and* **Finty** *clip themselves in.*

Tug (*shouting over the noise*)   Wait, no, you can't just leave me here! At least let me borrow your satellite phone!

Charlie (*shouting back*)   What's that, Tuggy?

Tug (*shouting*)   I said don't leave me!

Charlie (*shouting*)   Sorry, no, I just can't hear you over the sound of the magnificent rotor blades! Goodbye, Tuggy!

Charlie *gives a thumbs-up to the pilot, and* **Charlie** *and* **Finty** *start to ascend.*

Finty (*ascending*)   *Do svidanyia!*

Charlie (*ascending*)   *Do svidanyia!*

They board the helicopter.

Tug (*shouting over the noise*)   No! Come back! You need me! All of you need me! You don't understand! I'll explain it all! I'll explain everything!

He delivers a long, angry, on-the-nose, explicatory speech about the necessity of the aristocracy, but is completely drowned out by the exiting helicopter. The sound of the rotor-blades recedes, just enough to catch the end of **Tug**'s *tirade.*

. . . so now you see, now you all know the point of all this, and you can all show me infinite acceptance and understanding!!

The helicopter has gone. Silence.

Mrs Hanratty   I don't think anyone heard any of that, sir.

Tug   No.

Silence. **Tug** *and* **Mrs Hanratty** *remain, in the quiet.*

Tug   Well, then, Mrs Hanratty. You don't happen to have a vast fortune hidden away somewhere, do you? Bunch of Bitcoin stashed in an old Bovril jar? Undiscovered Rembrandt up in the attic? Cheeky Fabergé egg behind the sofa?

Mrs Hanratty   I do not.

Tug   Shame. I was thinking of asking you to marry me.

Mrs Hanratty   It's a proposal I'd have courteously declined on account of your being an enormous bell-end.

Tug   Oh, well, you'd be making a big mistake. I'm quite the catch, I'll have you know. I've got a castle.

Mrs Hanratty   I've heard it's looking a bit run down, these days.

Tug   Oh, I wouldn't say that. It just needs a bit of imagination.

Tug *goes over to a piece of rubble wall and makes a clumsy attempt to rebuild it. He gives up.*

No, I'm not going to do that.

He sits down.

You don't have any ketamine, do you, Mrs Hanratty?

Mrs Hanratty   No, but I think there's some spare sausage rolls over there. (*Points.*)

Tug   Lovely.

Tug *fetches the sausage rolls, sits down next to* **Mrs Hanratty** *and gives one to her.*

Mrs Hanratty   Thank you.

They eat the sausage rolls for a bit.

Tug   So, I hope you've ironed your cycling Lycra, Mrs Hanratty. It's the Deliveroo for me and you.

Mrs Hanratty   Well, probably not for you, sir.

Tug   Probably not, no. I wonder if there are any hardship funds for viscounts?

Mrs Hanratty   I believe they're called agricultural subsidies, sir.

Tug   Still, I don't much fancy my chances in the long term, to be honest.

Mrs Hanratty   I don't much fancy mine either, sir. Nor in the short term neither.

Tug   How so?

Mrs Hanratty   I'm afraid that assassin might have a little bit, well, you know . . .

She removes her blanket to reveal the spreading stain of a serious gunshot wound.

Shot me.

Tug (*standing, suddenly panicked*)   Oh, goodness, Mrs Hanratty, why didn't you say so before? Oh, God. Let me see if I can find you something. I'm sure there are some bandages or painkillers or something lying around here somewhere, oh, God!

Mrs Hanratty   There's nothing. I've checked.

Tug   Well, let me run out to the road, then! I can try and flag down a tractor or something!

Mrs Hanratty   You'd be too long. I've done all I can, Theodore, it's all right. (*Shifting a bit.*) I did a brief combat first aid course when I ran with the Baader-Meinhof boys back in the eighties, so I know a fatal gunshot wound when I see one. I don't have long left, and the sun will be down soon. Just sit with me for a bit.

Tug *looks around, anxious, thinking.*

Mrs Hanratty   Please. Don't leave.

Tug   Okay.

He sits down.

Mrs Hanratty   You know, I arrived for my first day at Oxford hoping I'd be changing the beds for hard-working council estate kids, or earnest-sounding engineering students from Central America. But then I turned up and there you were. A literal fucking viscount. I thought you were the biggest twat on the face of the earth and I despised everything that you stood for.

Tug   And now?

Mrs Hanratty   Oh, I still think you're the biggest twat on the face of the earth and I still despise everything that you stand for. But. Well. You know. You never pretended to be anything else.

She shivers.

You wouldn't mind putting that blanket back over my shoulders, there, would you, Theodore? It's starting to get a bit nippy again.

Tug *replaces the blanket.*

Mrs Hanratty   You're a gentleman, Theodore. Thank you.

She breathes and smiles.

This country is endlessly ridiculous. That's why I love it. I'd change almost everything about it, if I could. But maybe not that.

She looks at the sunset.

Look, there's the sunset now.

She starts singing the Soviet national anthem:

(*Singing.*)
    Through tempests the sunshine of freedom has cheered us,
    Along the new path where great Lenin did lead,

Tug *joins in:*

Mrs Hanratty *and* **Tug** (*singing*)
    Be true to the people, thus Stalin has reared us,
    Inspired us to labour and valorous deed!
    Our army grew up in the heat of grim battle,

Mrs Hanratty *closes her eyes.*

Tug (*continues singing, alone*)
    Barbarian invaders we'll swiftly strike down,
    In combat the fate of the future we'll settle,
    Our country we'll lead to eternal renown!

Silence. The last daylight fades over the ruins. **Tug** *looks out into the stillness.*

Do you feel that, Mrs Hanratty? Peace.

Enormous thanks to:

Vicky Featherstone, for the courage.

Everyone at the Royal Court Theatre.

The team: Amy, Nat, Karina, George, Laurie, Philipp, Fenella, Milla, Natasha, Chris, Malik, Aneesha, Penny, Chris, Jules, Tash, and Julia.

Rachel Taylor and Helena Clark.

Various valuable readers: Alistair McDowall, Daran Johnson, Lucy Morrison, James Macdonald, Jane Fallowfield, Gurnesha Bola, Ellie Fulcher, Chris James.

Tom and Sue. Zelda and Ned. Lucy, my person, always, always.

Sam Pritchard, my wonderful friend, this one's for you.

RM

Printed in the USA
CPSIA information can be obtained
at www.ICGtesting.com
LVHW011220150324
774517LV00047B/2252